Country to Campus

From Bureau County to Notre Dame: 1860s America

Timothy A. Schlindwein

ISBN: 979-8-9886941-1-3

Cover design by: Timothy A. Schlindwein

On the Cover:

Top Photo – View of Princeton, Illinois. As seen from the (railroad) North-West.
Published Isaac B. Smith 1857. Library of Congress

Bottom Photo – Sacred Heart Church & Main Building, ca. 1866
University of Notre Dame Francis P. Clark Collection 48-16-02

Printed in the United States of America

Contents

Foreword

A journey of discovery began with a chance remark amidst the 2020 pandemic. It came in a conversation between two childhood friends, Rebecca Best, great granddaughter of Lewis Thompson, and Jill Huffstodt, fourth cousin of Cyrus Fetrow. These two women are my wife Jill and her friend Becky, and this work is dedicated to them. This journey begins with Lewis, the first young man from Princeton, Illinois, to attend the University of Notre Dame. I followed him 102 years later.

Historical fiction depends on the history from which stories can be drawn. The stories here reflect a wide range of available public information. Gratitude and appreciation go to several institutions and professionals whose resources and assistance brought forth rich histories. Athens-Limestone (AL) Public Library; Limestone County (AL) Archives (Rebekah Davis); Limestone County Historical Society (Kathryn Davis); Bureau County (IL) Historical Society (David Gugerty and Mike Hult); Bureau County (IL) Genealogical Society (Esther Tracy); Princeton (IL) Public Library; City of Princeton, IL (Erik Ellberg); St. Mary's College Archives (Eric Walerko); University of Notre Dame Archives (Joe Smith). Judith Gosse and Jan Gosse shared records from their family archives.

A special thank you to Rebekah Davis, who served as both editor and publisher. Of course, any deficiencies are attributable to the author.

Introduction

During the years 1863 through 1869, eight young men from Bureau County, Illinois, attended the University of Notre Dame. It would be 21 years before another Bureau County student enrolled and 57 more years until the next young man attended. What drew this cohort of students to Notre Dame in the 1860s? Notre Dame advertised far and wide as early as the 1850s. Its advertisements appeared frequently in a local Princeton paper. A network of Catholic clergy traveled throughout the Old Northwest at this time, spreading the educational opportunities at Notre Dame. As shown in an advertisement from the New York Tablet of October 1, 1859, Notre Dame appealed to a Christian audience at large. All eight of the young men from Bureau County were Protestant Christians.

The eight Notre Dame students from Bureau County traveled different paths before university and their subsequent life experiences varied markedly. They followed a generation of true pioneers, entrepreneurs and risk-takers. They benefited from this generation but, in some ways, lived in its long shadow. Viewing the life paths of these students and those of their families provides a window to the passages of immigrants to and within the U.S. in the early decades of the 1800s. It also provides a view to major events and developments in both the country and the region as they played out through the second half of the 19th Century. Much has changed for small towns, universities, and the world generally since their time. Yet, the core dreams and aspirations of young men and women leaving the familiarity of home, family, and friends for the unknown challenges and opportunities of a distant university perhaps has changed little. A sense of continuity from this time emerges as we trace these distant journeys from country to campus, and beyond.

Sacred Heart Church & Main Building, ca. 1866
University of Notre Dame
Francis P. Clark Collection 48-16-02

UNIVERSITY OF NOTRE DAME.—ST. JOSEPH'S COUNTY, INDIANA. This Institution, chartered in 1844, numbers at the present time, in connection with St. Mary's, one mile distant, more than five hundred inmates. It is seated in the valley of St. Joseph, a region, one of the healthiest and most invigorating to the constitution in the northwest, between two railroads, either of which places is within thirty hours travel of New York or Philadelphia and within three of Chicago. The students are divided into four distinct Departments, viz: the Collegiate Department, comprising a full course in the Liberal Arts and Exact Sciences, has a corps of able Professors, mostly European. The Commercial, which has hitherto been the largest, is in the hands of competent and experienced Professors chiefly American. The Preparatory is designed to fit Students for the College proper and comprehends thorough Rudimental Instruction. The Department of the Minims contains twenty-five of the youngest boys, of ages ranging from six to ten years, and is exclusively under the charge of an American lady.

The discipline of the Institution though mild and easy is regarded as the main foundation of success both for teacher and pupil. A peculiar advantage of NOTRE DAME, as a place for Christian Education, is its retirement and seclusion from the moral contagion of large cities. Full of life as it is, it has yet a life of its own—an atmosphere of Catholicity, which a child rarely breathes elsewhere.

It is unnecessary to call the attention of Parents having sons and daughters to educate, to the proximity to the University, of St Mary's Academy, under the direction of the Sisters of the Holy Cross.

In both Institutions, the French and German are taught by natives of France and Germany.

TERMS, $125 PER ANNUM.

REV. E. SORIN, President.

NOTRE DAME, Jan. 1, 1859. my14 6m

Advertisement in the NY Tablet, January 1, 1859
University of Notre Dame Archives
Printed Materials Collection 1052-1850

View of Princeton, Illinois. As seen from the (railroad) North-West.
Published Isaac B. Smith 1857.
Library of Congress

Lewis K. Thompson

Rebecca usually looked forward to the renewal of spring after another harsh winter on the plains of northern Illinois. This spring, however, brought more reflection than renewal. Rebecca thought of the early days with her husband, Lewis K. Thompson, as she prepared to lay him to rest on this fourth Monday of April, 1912. Lewis had passed early Saturday evening in the family's Princeton, Illinois, home. The doctors had said his affliction was Bright's disease, identified in England eighty-five years earlier and associated with kidney-related ailments. In an early morning moment of quiet, the widow Thompson's thoughts drifted back to her Alabama home and her life before Lewis. He was neither her first husband nor, perhaps, her first love. But he was her rescuer from a life of challenges.

Rebecca Boshart knew well life's challenges. She was born May 3, 1843, in Marshall County, Alabama. She was the fourth of five children, with three sisters and one brother. Her father, Rudolph, died in 1850 at age 31, leaving her mother, Cynthia, to raise and support the family. Such circumstances would have been challenging at any time, but particularly for a family in rural America in the mid-1800s. Fortunately for Rebecca, her aunt, Nancy Boshart Rice, assumed responsibility for her care.

Nancy Boshart was only 17 years old when she married the 33-year-old William C. Rice on November 8, 1829, in Lawrence County, Alabama. William was a successful confectioner in the county, which was named for James Lawrence, the man remembered for exclaiming, "Don't give up the ship!" in the War of 1812.

Under Nancy's care, Rebecca caught the eye of a resident of

Athens in neighboring Limestone County. Hiram A. Higgins was the son of a prominent architect, Hiram H. Higgins. At age 15, Rebecca married Hiram, age 23, on December 15, 1858, at the home of her aunt and uncle, Nancy and William Rice. Two years later, Hiram was working as a railroad conductor.

The Civil War disrupted the lives of the citizens of Athens, particularly when the town and surrounding area were occupied in May 1862 by regiments of the Union Army, the 19th and 24th of Illinois and the 37th of Indiana. The occupation was so infamous for initial treatment inflicted by soldiers on civilians, their property and persons, that it became memorialized as "The Rape of Athens."

Hiram Higgins enlisted in the Confederate States Army at nearby Huntsville, Alabama, on October 10, 1862. He joined Captain Ward's Battery, Alabama Light Artillery. By the spring of 1863, he had attained the rank of corporal. That same year, William Rice died, and Nancy and Rebecca laid him to rest in the Athens City Cemetery. After four years of marriage, 19-year-old Rebecca and her widowed aunt were left alone in Athens under Union Army occupation.

Lewis was bound for college. The Chicago, Burlington & Quincy line, authorized by the state of Illinois in 1854, significantly reduced what had been a full-day trip from Princeton to Chicago, and Lewis Thompson embraced the new technology. In late August 1863, Lewis settled in for the 109-mile, four-hour train ride on the CB&Q. He thought of his family and friends left behind and wondered of the great adventure yet ahead. On September 1, he would begin his studies at the University of Notre Dame, and he would celebrate his 19th birthday fifteen days later.

What would draw this young man from his Illinois farmland home to a relatively new university in north central Indiana? Was it self-direction, encouragement from his parents, guidance from local clergy, or some of each influence? Growth in the South Bend, Indiana, area soon would put its population at twice that of

Princeton, but the much larger Chicago was the natural choice for a young man's bustle and adventure.

With the War now in its third full year, no end in sight, and casualties mounting, even the most patriotic 19-year-old could be inclined to steer clear of military service. Legal remedies were provided to forego such service, including paying a $300 commutation fee or enlisting a substitute. Lewis did not serve in the Union Army. Attending a university far from the War's front lines appealed to parents seeking safety for their oldest son. A safe distance from the distractions and pitfalls of the Chicago metropolis weighed in Notre Dame's favor as well. Notre Dame aggressively marketed its strengths nationally. They included a classic European education, a very disciplined and structured regimen for all activities, and a strong Christian heritage. The university welcomed students of all faiths and, in spite of its deep Roman Catholic traditions, the majority of students in those years were Protestant Christians, including Lewis and the seven young men from Princeton who followed him in successive years.

Lewis made his connection in Chicago to the Michigan Southern & Northern Indiana train that would take him the 85 miles to South Bend. While immersed in his thoughts, he soon realized that many fellow passengers who boarded in Chicago were of his age and headed for Notre Dame as well. This was his first encounter with soon-to-be classmates. With the first leg of his trip complete and the transfer in Chicago behind, he relaxed a bit, though not completely. Closing his eyes, he recalled reports of the terrible train wreck of 1841 that had occurred on this same line very near South Bend. Some reports said that more than 100 passengers perished.

The three-hour ride from Chicago to South Bend ended soon enough. Lewis disembarked and, along with his fellow student passengers, boarded the omnibus that would take them the last two miles to the Notre Dame campus. It had been a long journey, but Lewis' emotions ran high as he set foot on this campus, first opened in 1842. Who would he meet? How challenging would his classes be? Would he make it through almost a full year before returning home? He was here now, ready to undertake an opportunity few would experience. He was grateful.

Lewis was the first son born in the United States to Joseph V. Thompson and Mary E. Kent Thompson, both immigrants from England. Milo Township, Illinois, was still five years away from becoming an official township when Lewis was born there on September 16, 1844. Milo was one of twenty-five townships in Bureau County, and there the Thompson family farmed the county's fertile land. The Bureau County seat, Princeton, was a city known for its progressive views on providing quality education. Lewis attended the Princeton Union School, the predecessor of what would become the oldest township high school in Illinois.

Lewis settled into college life and undertook a full academic and extracurricular regimen in his year at Notre Dame. He took to the stage as an active member of the Thespian Society, performing roles in both plays at the evening commencement exercises on June 22, 1864. In Shakespeare's historical play, Henry IV, Part I, he represented Henry Percy, 1st Earl of Northumberland, 4th Baron Percy.

While over four centuries removed in time, Lewis could muster some affinity with the 1st Earl, whose mother was Mary of Lancaster. Lewis' own father was born in Lancashire in 1814. While the Earl rebelled against King Henry, Joseph Thompson's quieter rebellion was taking permanent leave of his homeland itself. Both the Earl and Joseph lost their first wives and remarried. Lewis' memories of his mother were strong as he occupied only-child status for three years before the birth of his full brother and her death six months later.

The second evening exercise performance was the amusing drama, Rory O'More. This work by Samuel Lover, Irish songwriter, composer and novelist, and portrait painter, originally was written as a ballad. Lover was a contemporary and business partner of Charles Dickens. He began an extensive trip of North America in 1846, traversing from New Orleans to Canadian provinces on a path through the Old Northwest. He died just four years after the performance of his play at Notre Dame.

Rory was an historical figure, one of the principal organizers of the Irish Rebellion of 1641, and a member of the Irish Catholic Confederacy. He was a leader of the ill-fated attempt to capture Dublin Castle and bring a quick and bloodless victory. However, the Rebellion marked the beginning of a decade of strife with extensive loss of life. Lewis represented Bill Jones in the play.

The play was popular, having a long run of 109 nights at London's Adelphi Theatre in 1837, and performed throughout England and the U.S. in the years since. The play's mixture of passions, declarations of love, willingness to die for country, friendship, and honor struck themes that resonated strongly with Lewis and his classmates as the American Civil War had entered its fourth year.

While both North and South felt the toll of the War economically and financially, Notre Dame continued to grow in its second decade. By 1853, student enrollment had reached 99 students, representing 12 of 31 states. A decade later, the roll for the school year 1863-1864 totaled 364 students. They represented 24 of 35 states, the District of Columbia and two foreign countries (Canada and Ireland). Geographic and socio-economic diversity enriched both the educational and life experiences across the student body.

Twenty-two students were from three states of the Confederacy. While loyalty to family and community was undiminished, students found a path to harmony that kept differences to quarrels and left bloodshed on the battlefields. Perhaps one unifying factor was the extensive and heroic actions of members of the Notre Dame religious community. Every student knew someone in the community who was in service to the Union Army as a chaplain or a nurse.

Lewis enrolled in Notre Dame's Commercial Course with an emphasis on bookkeeping. In this course, students would be given a diploma for completing the course, passing a satisfactory examination before the university's Board of Examiners, and giving clear evidence of their moral character. Students who did not pursue graduation could adopt a partial or irregular course, fitting them for commercial life or for any non-learned profession requiring special training. The course ran parallel with the full University course, and included all the advantages, literary and otherwise, which Notre Dame offered.

Lewis excelled with honors in bookkeeping theory and high honors in bookkeeping execution. He participated in modern languages as well, achieving honors in German. However, his studies at Notre Dame ended after one full year. He returned to Princeton and Bureau County, Illinois, without a diploma but further prepared to pursue his chosen career.

The Civil War struck northern Alabama and Limestone County quite hard as the area remained under occupation longer than any other. In April 1862, the Army of the Ohio, under the command of General Ormsby M. Mitchel, moved south from Kentucky with the goal of controlling all of northern Alabama. By May, Mitchel pronounced, *"All of Alabama north of the Tennessee River floats no flags but that of the Union."*[1] Following the issuance of the Emancipation Proclamation in January 1863, a "freedman's camp" was set up on 1,800 acres of the Hobbs Plantation, located in south Limestone County on the east bank of the Tennessee River.

On March 3, 1865, an act of the U.S. Congress formally established the Bureau of Refugees, Freedmen, and Abandoned Lands ("Freedmen's Bureau"). The purpose of the Freedmen's Bureau was to provide relief services to emancipated African Americans and other refugees of the Confederate States who were displaced by the War.

Circumstances brought two Harris families with pre-Revolutionary War lineage to Milo Township. Joseph W. Harris was born January 16, 1819, in Valley Falls, Rhode Island, into a longstanding New England family. His grandfather and namesake served in the U.S. Revolutionary War and was infamous as one of the disguised patriots who boarded English vessels to throw tea into Narragansett Sound. Joseph migrated to Bureau County in May 1840 by way of Michigan, where he had farmed. He bought land and farmed in Milo, the southernmost township in Bureau County, and ultimately took up residence in Tiskilwa just to the north.

With long family roots in Virginia, Michael Harris' family emigrated to Knoxville, Tennessee, where he was born in 1818.

Joseph and Michael answered the early call for enlistment in the Union Army. They could have been mistaken as brothers, for they each enlisted in October 1861 and were mustered into the 57th Illinois Infantry Company F in Chicago on December 26, 1861, Joseph as a corporal and Michael as a first lieutenant. The 57th saw fierce fighting, including the Battle of Shiloh, Tennessee, in April 1862 and the first Battle of Corinth, Mississippi, in May 1862. Both battles resulted in Union victories, but at high cost. Shiloh recorded the greatest number of casualties to that point in the War. The 57th recorded 187 men killed, wounded or missing. Joseph was wounded at Shiloh but continued on to the engagement at Corinth. Michael was wounded at Corinth and succumbed to disease from his wounds July 24, 1862. Reports of these outcomes reached Milo Township and were a source of both mourning and reflection for all neighboring families, including the Thompsons and their son Lewis.

Joseph served beyond the end of the War and was mustered out in July 1865. His last assignment was to the Freedmen's Bureau, where he was in charge of the headquarters at the Hobbs Plantation. Joseph had oversight over about 3,000 freedmen. The Bureau pursued a broad mandate, including education, healthcare and employment, the latter often on the very plantations on which they previously were enslaved.

Thomas Hubbard Hobbs was a native of Limestone County, born April 19, 1826. His family migrated from Virginia and had a history of service to the country. His grandfather served as a Captain in the War of 1812. Thomas left his home to earn a Bachelor of Arts degree from the University of Virginia and a law degree from the University of Pennsylvania, and then he returned to Limestone County to tend to the business of the Hobbs Plantation. Thomas was active in Alabama state government, first as a member of the Legislature. He was asked to run for governor, but he turned his efforts to secession.

Thomas raised the first company of soldiers in the county, and he entered the Confederate Army as Captain of Company F, 9th Alabama Infantry. The Company was dispatched to Richmond, Virginia. Thomas made one more trip home to recruit additional soldiers in February 1862. While serving in Virginia, notes in his own journal for June 4, 1862, record, *". . . heard today of the destruction of my house and the devastation of my farm by Dutch Yankees of General Mitchel."*[2] This notation about Slopeside, Thomas's farm on the Hobbs Plantation, was one of his last journal entries. Thomas was wounded in the Seven Days Battles near Richmond, and he died of his wounds on July 22, 1862.

At War's end, it was reported that no standing fence, stock or provisions were left on Slopeside Farm. All that remained was the shell of the farmhouse and the denuded land.

Duty, opportunity, adventure, or some of each. What drew Lewis Thompson to the post-War South in the spring of 1865? Lewis could not escape the sense of duty instilled by the service of Joseph Harris and Michael Harris, particularly when it was juxtaposed with Lewis' own lack of military service during the War. Lewis also recalled the heroism of the brothers and sisters of Notre Dame and St. Mary's as they served soldiers in need, mostly Union but Confederate as well.

Since attending Notre Dame, Lewis had been working in the field for which he was educated, bookkeeping. He had completed one full year with Fisher & Company, the largest trading company in Bureau County. Opportunities for commercial gain and career advancement seemed more favorable in the victorious Northern states.

Nurtured by his Notre Dame experience, a sense of adventure was growing within Lewis.

Athens, Alabama, was a growing city before the Civil War. Prominent individuals knew each other, and personal friendships and business engagements tied many together. Among this group were family names including Hobbs, Pryor, Rice, and Higgins.

Friendships forged before the War became even more important as Limestone County began its climb from occupation. Luke Pryor II was a close friend and collaborator of Thomas Hobbs, serving together in the Alabama legislature in the 1850s and cosponsoring important legislation. Pryor remained a community leader as well as a lawyer, farmer, and a member of both the U.S. Senate and House. He knew well of the Hobbs Plantation before, during, and after the War.

The Pryor, Hobbs, and Rice homes were in close proximity, and the Higgins home was but a few blocks distant. These families experienced the trauma of war firsthand, as troop engagements occurred in their very neighborhoods during the capture of Athens in 1862. With William Rice deceased and Hiram A. Higgins in distant service of the Confederate Army, Nancy Rice and her close niece, Rebecca Boshart Higgins, found company and support in each other.

Lewis Thompson traveled to Decatur Junction, Alabama, in May 1865 to join the service of the Freedmen's Bureau under the leadership of Lieutenant Joseph Harris on the Hobbs Plantation. The Freedmen's Bureau faced a staffing shortage with dwindling military personnel after the War's end. Lewis' education and experience with both business and agriculture made him valuable to the Bureau for the next two years. He then found employment on a cotton plantation for an additional year. While certainly a Yankee, Lewis was a bright, energetic young man who had come to Limestone County to help. Rebecca Higgins confided to Nancy Rice that she had been unhappy in her marriage for some time. The widow Nancy conjectured that an introduction of age-appropriate Lewis to Rebecca might provide a path to a brighter future for all three.

Hiram A. Higgins had seen duty as part of Captain Ward's Battery in campaigns crossing Alabama, Georgia and Tennessee, but the Battery was captured in Selma, Alabama, on April 2, 1865. Higgins surrendered in Athens, Alabama, May 15, 1865, and then traveled to Nashville, Tennessee, where he swore an oath of allegiance to the United States on June 1, 1865.

Rebecca Higgins knew she was going against the societal norms and mores of the 1860s that looked with disapproval on divorce generally and divorce pursued by women specifically. Still, she summoned her courage, and on May 27, 1867, Rebecca filed a petition for divorce at the Court of Chancery for the 28th District of the Northern Chancery Division of the State of Alabama. With a Respondent as prominent as Hiram A. Higgins, this trial was an area sensation.

Rebecca claimed that she was abandoned in October 1862 without any means to sustain herself and that Hiram had contributed nothing to her support. She further claimed that he was a habitual drunkard, that he had committed adultery (one such occurrence purported at a house of ill fame in Nashville), that he had habitually been negligent and disrespectful, that he had no property, that they had not lived together nor cohabited since he abandoned her, and that they had no children. She provided depositions from eight individuals, including her aunt, Nancy Rice.

Hiram filed his own petition on that same day, claiming his marital fidelity. He stated that he enlisted as a soldier in the Confederate Army in June 1862. He represented that his wife had forfeited his love and respect by the commission of acts incompatible with the fidelity and honorable duties of a wife. Specifically, she had lived in adultery with one Lieutenant Medow of the Union Army over undocumented dates. Further, she associated with and frequently appeared in public with men in a manner unusual for a married woman. He asserted that she admitted her adulteries. He further claimed that he filed this complaint with this same court nearly three months earlier, on March 7, 1867. He provided depositions from eight individuals, including Nancy Rice and Lewis K. Thompson.

As a witness for the Respondent, Lewis was not called to attest favorably to Rebecca's character. Rather, his testimony was to give witness to her infidelity, which would have pulled into the proceedings the nature of their own relationship. This tactic did not sway the outcome. A decree granting divorce was entered May 30, 1867, with Hiram directed to pay court costs.

With the weight of divorce proceedings lifted, Rebecca Boshart Higgins and Lewis K. Thompson were married just four days later, on June 3, 1867.

Lewis and Rebecca Thompson returned to Bureau County early in 1868. The Thompson family farming operations had migrated over time from modest beginnings in Milo Township at the south end of the County to a sprawling 479 acres in Walnut Township to the north. Standing at their new home at the southern edge of the expanse, the new couple gazed over an impressive vista of rich, rolling farmland. They dreamed of and hoped for their new life together, now removed from the War and its aftermath. Waiting ahead were seven children, commercial success, public service, travel, and nearly 45 years of marriage.

Rebecca's aunt, Nancy Boshart Rice, relocated from Athens, Alabama, as well, joining the Thompson household in Walnut Township. She had lost her spouse, suffered economic setback from the War, and was ostracized from the Athens elite for supporting her niece and aligning with a Yankee. In a letter to Alabama friends, she expressed her thoughts about her life change, saying, *"This is a fine country and very healthy, a good part of world for the farmer."*[3] Provisions for Lewis in Nancy's last will and testament revealed her feelings for this man, *". . . all my debts and money due me from L. K. Thompson be cancelled."*[4] She died in 1880 at age 68 and was laid to rest in the Thompson family plot at Oakland Cemetery in Princeton, Illinois.

Lewis K. Thompson passed on April 20, 1912, leaving no will or last testament. Rebecca petitioned the Bureau County Court to appoint her as administratrix of his estate, and her request was granted. It was a modest estate, and her five surviving children assigned any of their claims to their mother. Rebecca Boshart Thompson passed on March 21, 1923, and was laid to rest next to her husband in Oakland Cemetery.

Joseph V. Thompson amassed sizable real estate holdings in his lifetime. His management of them as well as their disposition after his passing tell two stories.

Few pioneers achieved Joseph's success. His agricultural land holdings were in excess of 500 acres. His development land holdings included 95 lots in the city of Princeton. The value in current dollars was in excess of $2.1 million. Owners with agricultural estates of this size often transitioned to operators, and they sourced the labor needed beyond immediate family in two ways. The simplest was to hire laborers, some of whom became household residents as their tasks were many and their work hours long. They struck more complex relationships with tenant farmers. In the most common arrangement between landowner and tenant farmer, the tenant paid a share of the crops for the use of the land. In addition, the landowner might make loans to the tenant for the latter's procurement of seed, tools and livestock. Going rates of interest often were 10% or higher. At the time of his passing, Joseph was an active lender with 39 loans outstanding to a mix of agricultural and development borrowers. In current dollars, the total value of these loans was in excess of $700,000, equal to one-third of the value of his real estate holdings. He was a prudent risk-taker with a diversified portfolio.

The continuation of family businesses over successive generations always has been a challenge. The experience of the Thompson family suggests the challenge arises in land enterprises just as with commercial ones. Joseph was a self-made man. His ambition, entrepreneurial spirit and willingness to undergo hardships and take risks were obvious. He left all behind in England to undergo the arduous Atlantic crossing and then pushed on to the rugged conditions of the newly opened Northwest. These characteristics were not always of equal strength in the children or grandchildren of a successful patriarch. The modest value of Lewis' estate some 41 years after the settlement of Joseph's estate suggests this outcome befell the Thompson family. Lewis and Rebecca lived challenging lives to be sure, but they were aided in part by the accomplishments of Joseph. The outcome was the diminution of his material legacy.

Lewis K. Thompson, 1870.
Bureau County Historical Society, Princeton, Illinois
Immke Glass Plate Collection

Rebecca Boshart Thompson, 1870.
Bureau County Historical Society, Princeton, Illinois
Immke Glass Plate Collection

SLOPESIDE, THE HOBBS PLANTATION EIGHT MILES SOUTH OF ATHENS

Courtesy of the University of Alabama Libraries Special Collections

Thompson Farm 1875, Section 19,
Walnut Township, Bureau County, Illinois.
Photo by Author, 2021

THOMPSON FAMILY TREE

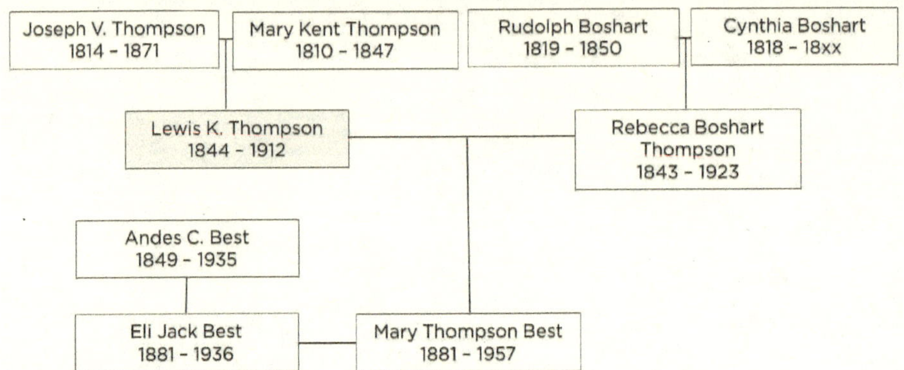

Cyrus J. Fetrow

In early September 1864, Cyrus J. Fetrow set off from Princeton, Illinois, to attend the University of Notre Dame. He followed the path that Lewis K. Thompson had first taken one year earlier. Their early life journeys, however, were quite different. Lewis was born in Bureau County, Illinois. Cyrus was born in York County, Pennsylvania. Lewis' parents migrated from their native England. Cyrus' parents were descendants of earlier German immigrants. However, Cyrus and Lewis had in common their Notre Dame experience and subsequent lives of interest, adventure, challenge and accomplishment.

John Phillip Fetrow and Johann Peter Hoffstadt were among the more than 65,000 Germans who migrated from the Palatinate area to America in the 1700s. They began travel from their homes, Heidelberg and Ellerstadt respectively. The Palatinate covered the lower regions of the Rhine River and was a natural pathway for conquerors such as Louis XIV of France. Such invasions over decades devastated the area and left inhabitants struggling for basic life necessities. Many died of starvation or exposure to the elements. As a result, they were quite willing to leave what little remained for travel to England under the perception that new opportunity awaited there or in her colonies.

William Penn played a role in the significant migration of Germans to his own colony of Pennsylvania. He traveled in the Rhine River Valley and delivered well-received messages of opportunity and religious tolerance. Pennsylvania became the largest home of German expatriates in America. These immigrants not only left their ancestral land, but also became

British subjects. England's struggle with France for global supremacy and her colonial expansion in America required many more loyal subjects, while not depleting their citizenry at home. From the 1720s to the 1770s, German immigrants found their way to Pennsylvania in more than 300 Atlantic Ocean crossings. The three-part journey to America was arduous: river travel up the Rhine to Rotterdam; transfer for ship passage to one of several English ports, often Cowe or Portsmouth; and the dangerous Atlantic crossing to the Port of Philadelphia, Pennsylvania.

Rumors did not exaggerate the hardship and danger of the Atlantic crossing. From Rotterdam to Philadelphia via Cowe was a four-month journey. A particularly tragic outcome befell a ship and its 400 Palatine passengers following this itinerary in late 1738. Far short of Philadelphia, the ship was cast away on Block Island off the coast of Rhode Island with only 105 survivors. In the end, only 90 survived a malignant fever that was traced to their only fresh water supply. It had been loaded at Rotterdam into casks previously filled with wine. The prospects of a better life in America compelled so many to face such hardships and take such risks.

Hostilities between England and France caused a complete suspension of German immigration from 1756 to 1761, but John Phillip Fetrow was able to make the journey before the suspension. Upon arrival in Philadelphia, he moved on to York County, Pennsylvania, and settled in Newberry Township. In 1754, he married a fellow German immigrant, Anna Mary Bose of Freudenstadt. She was thirteen years younger. By 1760, Mary had given birth to four boys, and John Phillip had obtained a land grant for 105 Newberry acres. Their family was completed by 1765 with another boy and their only daughter.

Johann Peter Hoffstadt and Mary Barbara Norton had married in their hometown of Ellerstadt, Germany, in 1743, she at age 20 and he at age 18. Delayed by the suspension of immigration, their journey to America began in June 1764. They set sail from Rotterdam on the ship Hero with their two young daughters and 496 other passengers. They disembarked at the Port of

Philadelphia on October 27, 1764. Johann Peter and Mary Barbara initially remained in the Philadelphia area, settling in Barren Hills to the northwest of the city, where Mary gave birth to their first son in 1765. The opportunities in the newly developing land to the west, and a cohort of immigrant countrymen already there, drew them on to York County, where their family was completed in 1777 with the birth of their second son.

Agrarian economies characterized the German homeland as well as the new land of York County. Large families generally were a blessing, as farm work was labor-intensive. Over three American-born generations, however, circumstances changed materially. In part due to large-scale immigration and a continuation of large family formations, initial opportunity had diminished. In addition, land value had appreciated significantly, so much so that individuals of means were the primary purchasers of land sold by original owners.

As land had drawn immigrants from Europe to colonial America a century earlier, more land carved out of the Old Northwest prompted migration in the 1800s to the new states. Opportunity arose not only for those who farmed the land, but also for those who provided necessary support – mills, mining, medical care, and more. All were entrepreneurs, taking great risks physically and financially in pursuit of opportunities to increase their quality of life.

From the early 1850s, members of the Fetrow and Hoffstadt families migrated from York County, Pennsylvania, to Bureau County, Illinois. In 1851, Johann Peter Hoffstadt's grandson, Peter Hoffstadt, arrived in Bureau County with his second wife, Barbara, and his son John. They settled on a farm southeast of Princeton.

Jacob Fetrow, great grandson of John Phillip, and Nancy Hoffstadt – daughter of Peter, sister of John, great-granddaughter of Johann Peter – were married on January 12, 1843, in Fairview Township, York County. Jacob had just turned 24 and Nancy soon would be 19. Their only child, Cyrus Jacob, was born four years later on July 6, 1847. Also in their household was Nancy's favored aunt, Barbara Hoffstadt, sister of Peter.

Jacob worked as a carpenter, but he aspired to something more. He migrated to Bureau County to further his pursuits. By 1855, Jacob and his family had established residence in Princeton. In 1857, Princeton was organized as a town and elected its first officers. Among them was Jacob Fetrow, elected as one of five fire wardens. Jacob's business pursuits were established as well as he became a lumber dealer, an important commodity as the town continued to grow.

Three of Jacob's brothers also migrated to Bureau County – Abraham, Yinger and Joseph. In time, and in his last years, their father, David, joined them. When David died in 1868, he was buried in Princeton's Oakland Cemetery.

Lewis Thompson returned to Princeton, Illinois, in the summer of 1864, following his year at the University of Notre Dame. Knowledge of his experience was helpful to Cyrus Fetrow as he prepared for the same educational opportunity. As Lewis before him, 17-year-old Cyrus boarded the eastbound Chicago, Burlington & Quincy ("CB&Q") train in Princeton destined for Chicago. Cyrus fully appreciated the modern convenience of rail travel. It had been but a few years since his family made the much longer, in distance and time, grueling overland trip to Princeton from Pennsylvania.

The CB&Q made 21 stops on the 109-mile ride from Princeton to Chicago. Villages, towns, and cities with stops on a major railroad line had a stronger growth opportunity than those serviced by lesser lines. Over time, competitive forces reduced an overcrowded railroad industry to a number of stronger survivors, stunting the growth of areas no longer serviced. No stop on the CB&Q benefitted more than Chicago, the emerging crossroads of America's east-west rail traffic. The growth of Chicago and its many opportunities were not lost on Cyrus, although, for now, he only was passing through.

Cyrus joined a Notre Dame student body that had grown a sizable 27% in one year to an enrollment of 463. Students represented 15 of 36 states, one territory (New Mexico), the District of Columbia and Canada. Enrollment from the Confederacy had grown as well to 41 students from four states. Clubs and societies formed in response to both university priorities and student interest. Some 60 students formed the Notre Dame Gymnastic Club that fall for their physical education.

Cyrus embraced a full academic and extracurricular regimen in his year at Notre Dame. He enrolled in the Commercial Course, with its broad curriculum that included Mathematics, English, Bookkeeping, Foreign Language, Geography, History, Commercial Law, Writing, and Elocution. Cyrus was an excellent student. He earned a Master of Accounts degree, one of 34 students receiving this degree at the commencement exercises on June 22, 1865. He received an overall Senior Department honor, an honor in Geometry, an honor in Commercial Law, a highest honor in Bookkeeping Theory, an honor in English Recitation, and an honor in English Composition. Fittingly, his foreign language was German. He studied Instrumental Music, where he was awarded an honor in his instrument of choice, the violin.

Because no Thespian Society was formed in the 1864 school year, no students performed the usual plays at the 1865 commencement exercises. Larger events playing out on the national stage also impacted the commencement program. The Civil War had ended on May 9, 1865, but the recovery for both North and South had just begun. Certainly, students from the former Confederate states approached the end of the school term and the return to their respective homes with some trepidation. President Abraham Lincoln, assassinated on April 15, 1865, was on the minds of all. Spirits rose in the days leading up to commencement in anticipation of the attendance of General William Tecumseh Sherman of the Union Army.

Cyrus did not serve in the Union Army. While volunteer service was an option, his parents feared this choice for their only child. To provide manpower for the Army, the U.S. Congress passed the Enrollment Act of 1863. It provided for the enrollment for service of all male citizens and immigrants who had applied for citizenship between ages 20 and 45. Cyrus turned 20 after the War's end.

With the arrival of General Sherman on campus, Cyrus' connections to the Battle of Shiloh grew to four of the Battle's veterans. The service of both Joseph Harris and Michael Harris at Shiloh was well known back in Bureau County, Illinois. Joseph and General Sherman were wounded at Shiloh following engagement in the 1862 siege of Corinth, Mississippi. Cyrus now knew a faculty member at Notre Dame who fought at Shiloh as well.

Timothy Edward Howard was a well-liked member of the faculty who taught courses in both Rhetoric and Mathematics during the 1864–1865 school year. Howard was born on January 27, 1837, to parents who had both immigrated from Ireland, and he experienced a challenging childhood in rural Michigan near Ann Arbor. Timothy was only 14 when his father died, leaving him to take responsibility for his seven siblings. However, he completed high school and was enrolled at the University of Michigan at age 18. Further family setbacks interrupted his education there, but still he found his way to Notre Dame in 1859.

Howard's studies were interrupted again as he entered the service of the Union Army, joining the 12th Regiment of the Michigan Infantry. Only one month after the Regiment was mustered in, it was engaged in the Battle of Shiloh. Howard was nearly mortally wounded, but he recovered at the military hospital in Evansville, Indiana, and returned to Notre Dame. Before the 1864 school year started, he married Julia Redmond of Detroit and they settled into life in South Bend, Indiana.

General Sherman and General Ulysses Grant were popular Civil War heroes. Fresh from decisive battles, they were in great demand for appearances across the country. One notable venue at which they both were scheduled to appear was the Chicago Northwestern Sanitary Fair of 1865. The need for funding to support sick and wounded soldiers of the Union Army became apparent early in the War. On June 18, 1861, the

U.S. Congress passed legislation that created the United States Sanitary Commission. This private relief agency received funds through many activities, including the Fair of 1865 and its smaller predecessor held in Chicago two years earlier. In April 1865, work began on the construction of a great hall. It completely covered Dearborn Park, located near the lakefront and at the heart of the city, bordered by Randolph Street, Washington Street, and Michigan Avenue. The Fair opened on May 30. Sherman appeared on June 8 and Grant on June 10.

General Sherman and Mrs. Sherman had close ties to Notre Dame generally, and especially to its founder and president, Reverend Edward Sorin, C.S.C. While Sherman himself was baptized as an adult, Mrs. Sherman was the fervent Catholic who came to value the education which Notre Dame could provide for her sons, and nearby St. Mary's College could provide for her daughters. For a period of time, she even took up residence in South Bend to be near the schools and her children in attendance. Sherman himself encountered nuns on the war front from St. Mary's and was impressed with their impact on his soldiers. Mrs. Sherman and Father Sorin collaborated on mutual interests, he to provide U.S. Army chaplains at her urging and she to assist with service exemptions for his clergy brethren when such was in political jeopardy. She was of the influential Ewing family of Lancaster, Ohio. Through her husband, her letters of pleadings for Sorin reached President Lincoln himself on Christmas Day 1864.

When the Notre Dame administration realized that General and Mrs. Sherman would pass through South Bend enroute by rail to Chicago on June 7, 1865, they made arrangements for them to visit campus. The reunion of the two Shiloh veterans, General Sherman and Professor Howard, was a special occasion for Cyrus and his fellow students to witness. Following the students' ovation for Sherman, Howard represented his fellow faculty in addressing him: *"We knew that General Sherman would come to see the places made sacred to him by the consecrating footsteps of his family, and rest with us and let Notre Dame be a gentle spot in midst of toils in the present and honors in the future."*[5] The Notre Dame field band, thirty-five students strong, traveled to Chicago to make a musical presentation for Sherman at the Fair.

General Sherman returned to the Notre Dame campus for commencement on June 22, 1865. As was his custom, he delivered unprepared remarks. Sherman commented on his own childhood and the self-reliance it had instilled in him. He was one of eleven siblings in a family that was shattered at the death of their father when Sherman was 9. A West Point graduate himself, he remarked to faculty, students, and guests that June day, *"Let me not forget that I was once a young man like those who have appeared before the audience on this day and occasion. You should be grateful that you are under such good instruction and guidance. You now have a pilot on board to guide you, but the time will come, and soon, when you will have to go forth into the great, dark seas alone, under your own guidance."*[6] Four years after his address at Notre Dame and under the presidency of Ulysses Grant, Sherman became the third General of the Army, preceded only by Grant and George Washington.

On June 24, the Chicago Tribune reported extensively on Notre Dame's 21st Commencement exercises and the address by General Sherman, as well as the commencement at St. Mary's that followed. The Shermans were in attendance that night and were proud parents. Their daughter was a St. Mary's student and performed a leading role in a featured commencement play. Another set of parents was proud as well, for listed among the degree recipients in the Chicago Tribune report was a familiar name, Cyrus J. Fetrow, Princeton, Illinois.

Cyrus departed on the same train to Chicago that had brought him to Notre Dame the prior September. He passed through the city in the closing days of the Northwestern Sanitary Fair. Then it was on to the CB&Q and the last leg of his journey home to Princeton and Bureau County. Many CB&Q trips lay ahead for Cyrus. For now, he was inspired by his year at Notre Dame and very well prepared for his life and career ahead.

Cyrus returned to the family home and the warm embrace of his parents. They doted over their only child, and he in turn was a dutiful son. Mentoring him in his business career was a high priority for his father, Jacob. He saw the value of his son's many talents, which were corroborated in his success at Notre Dame. Cyrus had another life goal to accomplish as well.

Susan Booton was born on February 10, 1850, in Knox County, Illinois, 70 miles southwest of Bureau County. Like counties in eight other states, Knox was named for Henry Knox, who directed the artillery under General George Washington. On June 29, 1857, Susan's mother, Narcissa, married her second husband, the widower Harvey North, in Knox County. Harvey took Narcissa and his new stepdaughter, Susan, back to Princeton, where he resided and was an established jeweler. Cyrus Fetrow and Susan Booton-North met and were married in Princeton.

Jacob Fetrow determined that his fortune and that of his growing family would be best pursued in the much larger city of Chicago. The population of Chicago had surpassed 200,000 and represented ten percent of Illinois' total population. Jacob, Nancy, Cyrus, Susan, and Barbara boarded the CB&Q and settled into their Cottage Grove Avenue residence on the City's south side. Jacob and Cyrus began the first of many working partnerships in which Cyrus used his bookkeeping skills, honed at Notre Dame, to manage financial matters.

By 1870, the firm Waring, Fetrow & Wells was in operation as agents for "earth closets" as composting toilets were known. The handling and disposition of human waste was an age-old challenge that was compounded in larger population centers such as Chicago. Of general concern was the impact on public health from mishandling. Even at this time, modern sewer systems facilitating disposal via indoor plumbing were out of reach for most. Prior to 1855, no sewage system had been established for the city. The contamination of the Chicago River from raw sewage continued for years. Earth closets patented in the United

States improved on installations first introduced in England. The advancement was the mechanization of the covering of human waste with absorbent earthen materials while awaiting proper removal. The Fetrows positioned themselves to profit from this new technology.

The Fetrows moved to a new residence at #6 Woodland Park. Woodland Park was one of two green spaces bounded by Cottage Grove Avenue to the west and Lake Michigan to the east. West of Cottage Grove Avenue and bounded by 34th Street to the south was the University of Chicago. The university occupied ten acres of land owned and donated in 1855 by Stephen A. Douglas, Abraham Lincoln's famous debater. This was a desirable neighborhood and a fortuitous location for what lay ahead. At this time, favor was with the Fetrows, as added to the household was 23-year-old Abbie Garen from Ireland, the Fetrow family's domestic servant.

The Fetrows would experience life's extreme highs and lows in the next few years. News of Susan's pregnancy with her first child was a moment of family celebration. Close in time, however, Susan returned to Princeton in April 1871 for the burial of her mother at Oakland Cemetery. Narcissa North was laid to rest beside husband Harvey North's first wife, Caroline. Harvey would join them both in 1873 at age 64.

Weather conditions throughout the middle western United States in the summer and fall of 1871 set the stage for the calamity that befell Chicago. A severe drought had continued for months. Combined with high temperatures and winds, large fires burned over wide stretches of forest and plain in upper Michigan and Wisconsin and across Minnesota. In the first week of October, many fires had broken out in Chicago, putting a strain on fighters and available equipment. A large fire broke out Saturday night, October 7, near the corner of Clinton and Van Buren streets. It spread a block north and two blocks east to the south branch of the Chicago River. Lumber and coal yards were engulfed and fueled the fire throughout Sunday. Unfortunately, the critical second fire on Sunday night, October 8, was mistaken at first as just a blazing up of the earlier fire's ruins. Pushed on by powerful winds and airborne embers that leaped the river, the second fire consumed the downtown, jumped the river again to the north, and continued on its path of devastation.

An eyewitness said, *"It was like a snowstorm only the flakes were red instead of white."*[7] It was not flames but solid walls of fire. The prominent Court House in the center of the city burned in twenty minutes. A city that many took as the epitome of urbanizing America was in fifteen short hours reduced to ruin.

The Fetrow family and their neighbors saw the flames, felt the heat, breathed the smoke-filled air, but were not at direct risk as the Great Fire left the south side of Chicago untouched. At the fire's end on October 10, the city was reeling from massive loss: 100,000 homeless; 2,000 acres and 17,500 buildings destroyed; an estimated 300 killed.

The days after the fire were gloomy ones. The city was without water, food, and gas. Homeless Chicagoans with their meager belongings sought shelter in open spaces like Woodland Park outside the Fetrow front door. Looting began even during the fire and required the help of military forces and the private services of Pinkerton's Preventive Police. Justice was swift. Anyone caught looting or suspected of looting was shot on sight. Railways issued free passes to anyone wanting to leave the city, and 5,000 departed on one train alone. The CB&Q provided passage west to Aurora and beyond to Princeton. The Fetrows, however, were determined to accept the current situation, and to remain and to work through to better times.

Even as the fire burned, a ray of hope for the future emerged. On the prairie to the west to which thousands of refugees fled, some forty children were born on the night of the fire. Two days later, the Fetrows were in great celebration themselves as Susan gave birth to a daughter, Lizzie Maude.

The fire's economic and financial consequences did impact Cyrus as, for the first time, he took employment away from Jacob. He became a bookkeeper for the S.H. Harris Company of Chicago, a maker of safes. Following the Great Fire, new demand for the protection provided by their large, heavy metal devices spurred company growth, even though the record of the fire was mixed. Of the thousands of safes taken from the fire, about half failed to protect their contents. Of the remaining not recovered, it was estimated that 90% failed. The demand for earth closets was strong, too, both for replacement and first-time purchase, and Jacob continued selling those as well.

While they survived the Great Fire and financial prosperity continued, the Fetrow family suffered a heavy loss in the Spring of 1872. Lizzie Maude died on May 31 at only 7 months, 19 days. The family accompanied her body on the CB&Q to Princeton, where she was buried in Oakland Cemetery beside her great-grandfather. Returning to Chicago once again and before year's end, Susan was pregnant with her second child. With the economic Panic of 1873 in view and lingering concerns over the possible contributing factors of Chicago's environment to Lizzie's demise, Susan retreated to Princeton. She gave birth there to a son, Thomas Chester, on July 21, 1873. The Fetrow family soon would be reunited at their 6 Woodland Park home.

Consumption, or what came to be named tuberculosis in 1832, had been a destructive disease throughout human history. The longstanding common name reflected the weight loss associated with this disease that generally attacked the lungs. It was an infectious disease passed from person to person through coughing, spitting, sneezing, or speaking. The disease's manifestation and progression would vary widely from person to person depending on other health conditions. Given the nature of its spread, the urgency of addressing the disease was heightened in more dense, urban population centers.

Cyrus Fetrow was struck by consumption. Living and traveling within Chicago, with its population passing 300,000, exposed him to many potential sources of the disease. In addition, many lung-related illnesses arose after the Great Fire, resulting in delay of diagnosis or treatment of consumption. A more rapid disease progression for Cyrus prompted him to record on March 26, 1874, his last will and testament. He identified three bequests: to his beloved wife, to his dear father, and to his dear son. He requested that his father have charge of his son's property until age 21 and that his father serve as executor. Cyrus died four days later, on March 30. The Fetrow family boarded the CB&Q to Princeton once again, and placed Cyrus at rest beside his grandfather and daughter. He was 26 years, 8 months and 25 days old. At his passing, Jacob remarked, *"... what had been his great loss was Cyrus' eternal gain."*[8] Remembrances of his father for Thomas Chester would be left to those shared by his mother, grandparents and great aunt in the years ahead.

The Fetrow family returned to 6 Woodland Park in Chicago. Even while in mourning, Susan, still young at age 24, had to think of the best path forward for her son, Thomas, and herself. While any further loss of family members would be painful, Jacob and Nancy understood her need. On May 13, 1878, Susan married William Woods Craddick, fourteen years older and a widower with two daughters of his own. Jacob and Nancy gave their blessing and opened their home for the wedding ceremony. Susan, Thomas, and William left Chicago for his home in Knoxville, Iowa, 40 miles southeast of Des Moines and over 300 miles from Chicago. In the years ahead, Susan would give birth to another son and daughter.

Jacob, Nancy, and Barbara moved forward without Cyrus, Susan, and Thomas. Jacob no longer could rely on his lifelong confidant. His business interests shifted to grain markets and real estate. He remained an entrepreneur, forming a series of partnerships with different collaborators and taking up offices at several locations in Chicago's central business district. He was drawn to one individual in particular, Edwin C. Day. Day portrayed many of Cyrus' attributes. He was of a prominent family in grain trading, and he had been college-educated in both the U.S. and Switzerland. Their collaboration extended over several years.

A double loss struck Jacob in 1884. His beloved wife, Nancy, died on June 17. Another train ride to Princeton and another burial in Oakland Cemetery followed, this time for Nancy at age 60. One month later, Nancy's aunt, Barbara Hoffstadt, a member of their household since earlier years in York County, Pennsylvania, passed as well. Jacob now was alone for the first time in his life. His business activity continued with Edwin Day.

In May 1889, the news reached Jacob of Susan Fetrow Craddick's passing at age 39 in Knoxville, Iowa. His grandson, Thomas, was just shy of age 16. In the following months, Jacob gave thought to his own mortality and the need to make arrangements. He recorded his last will and testament on October 14, 1889. He identified specific bequests to two individuals. To Thomas would go a sizable amount of cash and extensive land holdings that Jacob had acquired in the part of Chicago's expansion to the northwest known as Irving Park. The residual of his estate was bequeathed to his beloved wife, Cassie R. Fetrow. In addition, he named her executrix of his estate.

Alone at 6 Woodland Park, Jacob had taken as his second wife Cassilda ("Cassie") Wert, a woman in her 20s who was 45 years his junior. Cassie had come to Woodland Park as a servant in Jacob's household. Jacob Fetrow died on January 19, 1891. His last will and testament also made provision that a sum of money was to be directed to the mayor of Princeton, Illinois, *"... and his successors forever ... for keeping in repair and ornamenting my lot in Oakland Cemetery ..."*[9] Cassie saw to it that this last wish of Jacob was fulfilled, and he made his final trip on the CB&Q to his resting place in the family plot at Oakland. However, Thomas' path to his inheritance proved more difficult.

One week shy of Thomas' 21st birthday, his guardian, J.S. Huey, filed suit in the Circuit Court of Chicago on July 14, 1893. The defendants were Cassie Krause, Jacob's widow, and her new husband, Russell Krause. They had been married the previous December in Chicago. The suit claimed that no proper accounting was made of the property held in trust for Thomas, and that both in Jacob's lifetime and after, property was sold, and Jacob and Cassie used the funds for their own benefit. The suit further claimed that Jacob had become of unsound mind and that Cassie had poisoned and influenced his mind against his grandson. In plain terms, Cassie was accused of *"exceptional sagacity, shrewdness and vivacity"*[10] which she exercised in *"many undue arts and fraudulent practices"*[11] to further her mercenary motives to capture Jacob Fetrow. As headlined in the Bureau County Tribune, *"It is The Old Old Story of An Old Man's Imbecility and a Woman's Wile."*[12]

Thomas Chester Fetrow married Alta Kinkead of Knoxville, Iowa, in Des Moines, Iowa, on October 30, 1895. He returned with Alta to Chicago, where their only child, Katherine, was born in 1900. Thomas and Alta lived full lives. Thomas built upon the remaining legacy to him which was born of his grandfather Jacob's love for his own son, Cyrus. The Fetrow name through this line of the family came to an end.

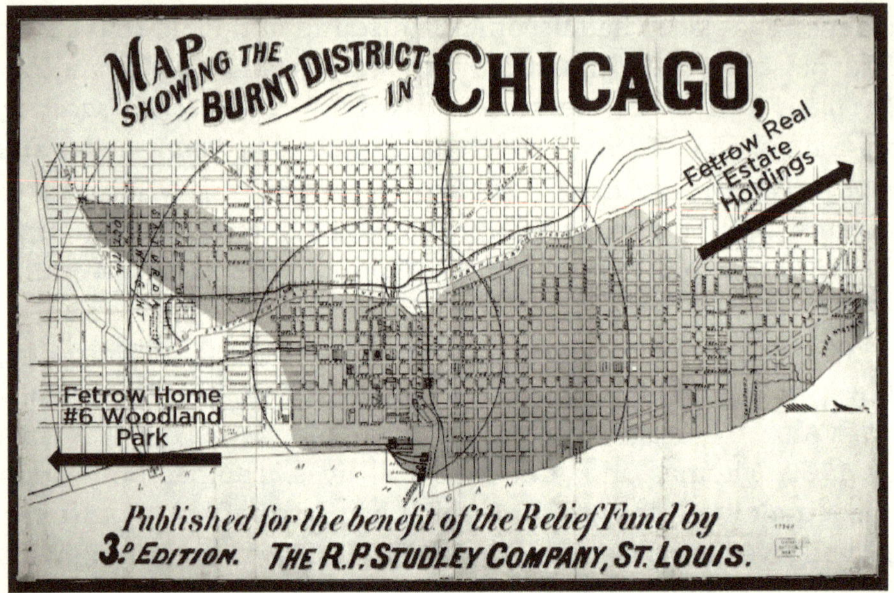

Map showing the burnt district of Chicago.
Chicago History Museum, ICHi-002870

Thieves & Burglars!

OFFICE OF

Pinkerton's Police.

Orders are hereby given to the Captains, Lieutenants Sergeants and Men of Pinkerton's Preventive Police, that they are in charge of the Burned District from Polk Street, from the River to the Lake and to the Chicago River. Any person Stealing or seeking to steal, any of the property in my charge, or attempt to break open the Safes, as the men cannot make arrests at the present time, they shall

Kill the Persons by my orders, no Mercy Shall be shown them, but Death shall be their fate.

Allan Pinkerton.

Notice to Thieves & Burglars from Allan Pinkerton's Police. Chicago History Museum, ICHi-037933

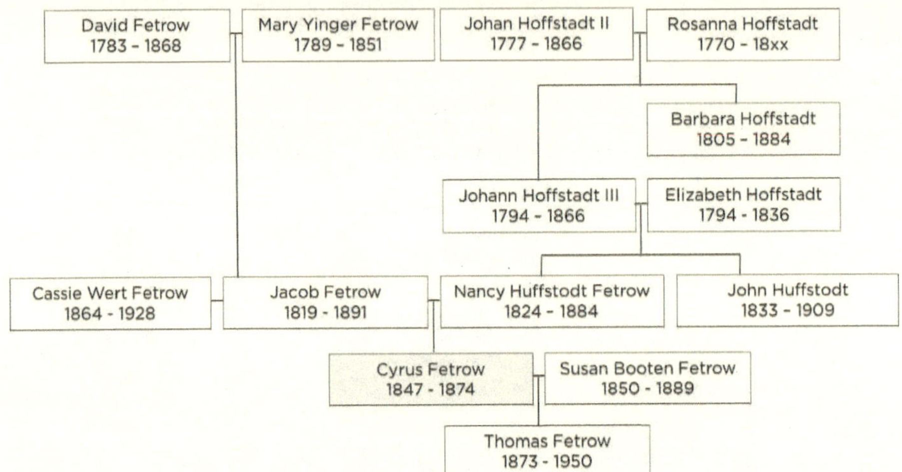
FETROW FAMILY TREE
David Fetrow
1783 - 1868
Mary Yinger Fetrow
1789 - 1851
Johan Hoffstadt II
1777 - 1866
Rosanna Hoffstadt
1770 - 18xx
Barbara Hoffstadt
1805 - 1884
Johann Hoffstadt III
1794 - 1866
Elizabeth Hoffstadt
1794 - 1836
Cassie Wert Fetrow
1864 - 1928
Jacob Fetrow
1819 - 1891
Nancy Huffstodt Fetrow
1824 - 1884
John Huffstodt
1833 - 1909
Cyrus Fetrow
1847 - 1874
Susan Booten Fetrow
1850 - 1889
Thomas Fetrow
1873 - 1950

Albert Knox

The attraction of abundant and inexpensive land and the promise of a new life drew the earliest settlers to Bureau County, Illinois. The hardiest of these agrarian entrepreneurs survived and word of their survival brought others. Some pursued agricultural opportunities as well, but many others sought the opportunities inherent in the development of whole new communities. They needed virtually everything, from goods to services, as none had existed before. They developed land, whether undeveloped prairie or converted farms, for homes, businesses, churches, and schools. There would be booms and busts, rivalries and alliances. Opportunity seekers entering Bureau County included the Knoxes of Highland County, Ohio, the Mercers of Frederick County, Virginia, and the Chritzmans of Dauphin County, Pennsylvania. These families were brought together by marriages and business ventures that produced many progenies and much commercial success. The 1837 marriage of William Knox and Mary Mercer brought eight children, the fifth of which was Albert, born November 25, 1846. It was he who would find his way to the University of Notre Dame.

Albert Knox enlisted and mustered into Company A of the Illinois 148th Infantry Regiment on February 7, 1865. The 148th was dispatched to various locations in Tennessee. Its primary service was guarding captured railways as the Union Army extended its control up to and through the end of the war. More men in the Regiment fell to disease than to bullets. Illness struck Albert early in his tour of duty. As a result, he saw limited active duty. Nevertheless, he reached the rank of corporal. He was mustered out of his company at Nashville, Tennessee, on September 5, 1865. Following a short trip home, Albert was on his way to Notre Dame.

Albert registered at Notre Dame on October 24, 1865. Reflecting in part the end of the Civil War, attendance had grown 9% from the prior year to an enrollment of 505. Students represented 19 of 36 states, one territory (New Mexico), the District of Columbia and Canada. Enrollment from the states of the former Confederacy declined by 15%. The majority of those attending were from Tennessee. Like Lewis Thompson and Cyrus Fetrow before him, Albert enrolled in the Commercial Course. Showing his interest in a broader education, he added German and music to his studies. With the combination of his experiences and exposures in the Union Army and at Notre Dame, Albert returned to Princeton, Illinois, in the summer of 1866 with a new appreciation of people, places, and opportunities for his life ahead.

Albert both benefited from and participated in his family's expanding relationships. The marriage of his parents joined the Knox and Mercer families, as did the marriage of William Knox's sister, Polly, to Mary Mercer's brother, William. The marriage of Albert's sister, Rachel, to Jacob Chritzman would lead to the launch of Albert's career. Albert's own marriage to Agnes ("Nellie") North reinforced his connection to Cyrus Fetrow, who had preceded him at Notre Dame. Agnes was the daughter of Morgan North and the niece of Harvey North, stepfather to Cyrus Fetrow's wife, Susan.

The City of Princeton was laid out in a traditional north-south, east-west grid pattern. Main Street divided the city east and west, while Peru Street (the road to Peru, Illinois, to the east) divided the city north and south. North Street and South Street originally defined approximately one quarter intervals either side of Peru Street, but their definition lost meaning as the city grew in all directions. In later years, North Street was renamed Central Street, indicating its more accurate positioning in the city layout. South Street was renamed Park Avenue, reflecting the many fine homes both east and west. The first sale of lots in the city began in May 1833. Credit was made available with six months interest payable upfront. Lots along Main Street were platted at one acre and were sold for an average of $2.50. The next lots back were platted at five and ten acres, with some as large as 40- and 80-acre tracts. Such tracts provided that farmland initially would continue in the city proper.

A natural progression for owners of large tracts in the city was development of the land for commercial and residential use. Both the Knox and Mercer families owned large tracts that were developed. Their farms were adjacent and comprised a good part of what was developed into the northwest section of Princeton. The Knox land included 371 acres that extended as far east as Main Street. The north boundary was the Chicago, Burlington & Quincy rail lines and train depot. In the 1870s, William Knox built a hotel at the northeast corner of his land, bordered by Main Street and the depot grounds. It was a substantial, three-story brick structure that included rental rooms and a dance hall. It was ideally located to service visitors to Princeton arriving by rail. The hotel operated under several names over the years, including Depot Hotel, National Hotel, Union Hotel, Hotel Powell and Knox Hotel.

The real estate activities of William Knox were similar to the earlier ones of Joseph Thompson. In addition to agricultural land holdings, William was directly involved in the development of land, including the aforementioned hotel. Joseph had been an investor in the American House, an early and sizable mixed-use building at the corner of Princeton's Main Street and the prominent courthouse square. The current dollar value of William's real estate holdings was in excess of $875,000. He was engaged in the business of lending as well. At his passing, outstanding loans were at a smaller scale, representing about 13% of the stated value of his real estate holdings. Interest rates on these loans ranged from 6% to 10%. Unfortunately, with respect to the soundness of the loans, most were identified either as "desperate" or "doubtful" while only a few were considered "good." Listed among the desperate borrowers was his own son, Oscar.

Jacob Chritzman learned his trade as a molder in Lancaster, Pennsylvania. He traveled west, first stopping in the State of

Minnesota, and ultimately settling in Princeton in 1855. He purchased an acre of land from William Knox that was bordered by the depot grounds and the rail lines. There he established a foundry operating as the Princeton Manufacturing Company. As his business grew, he relocated it to Main Street. He manufactured and sold a full range of farm implements and wagons. For many years, his was the largest business of its kind in Bureau County. Jacob was active in the civic life of Princeton as well. Princeton High School was the first in the country to operate under a special state charter. Enacted into law on February 5, 1867, the charter designated the first board of education, which included Jacob Chritzman. Albert Knox moved from farming to a sales position with his brother-in-law, Jacob.

Following their marriage on February 3, 1869, Albert and Agnes relocated to Afton, Iowa, where Albert sold the Chritzman products. Their only child, Elizabeth ("Bessie"), was born there in 1870. Agnes met an early death only one year later at age 27 and was laid to rest in Afton. Albert remained in Iowa for approximately ten years before returning to Princeton, where he moved in with Jacob and Rachel Chritzman. His employment continued with Chritzman, and he put his Notre Dame education to good use serving as the company's bookkeeper.

Albert courted and married Carrie L. Cade in Princeton on November 19, 1884. Carrie was 23 and 14 years younger than Albert. They enjoyed six years of marriage with no children before Carrie met an early death as well at age 29.

Having served in the Union Army, Albert took an active interest in the Grand Army of the Republic (the "GAR"). The GAR was a national fraternal organization composed of Union veterans of the Civil War. Founded in Decatur, Illinois, in 1866, the GAR was effective at lobbying for veteran benefits, advocating voting rights for African American veterans, establishing Decoration Day (renamed Memorial Day), and supporting political candidates, primarily of the Republican Party. It was organized around local community "posts." The Princeton post was #309. Albert traveled to GAR events within and outside of Illinois in the company of fellow veterans, including Andes Cordilla ("A.C.") Best.

A.C. Best was a manufacturer of headstones, monuments, and related cemetery work. Many of the monuments in Princeton's Oakland Cemetery were the work of his firm. Best was a close friend of Albert, serving as a pallbearer at the funeral of Albert's daughter, Bessie, who passed in Kansas City, Missouri, on May 11, 1919, at age 49. Friendships and linkages among the Notre Dame students of Princeton were typified by the friendship of Albert Knox and A.C. Best. Best would become father-in-law to Mary Thompson, daughter of Lewis (the first Notre Dame student from Princeton) and Rebecca Thompson, when she married A.C.'s son, Eli Jack.

Albert's propensity to travel took an adventuresome turn in the 1890s. With his oldest brother, Aaron, they relocated from Princeton to Hyattville, Wyoming, a small settlement in a scarcely populated part of the state west of the Bighorn Mountains. The Chicago, Burlington & Quincy Railroad transported them over 1,000 miles via Denver, Colorado, and Casper, Wyoming. The last 100 miles were overland. Their pursuit was mining, gold in particular. At their respective ages, they went not as miners themselves but as investors. Albert made a substantial investment in 17,800 shares of the Benzant Gold Mining Company.

Albert returned to Princeton and his business interests. It had been 17 years since Albert had a spouse when, in the Spring of 1907, he entered into marriage with Lillie Fisk Smith. This was her second marriage. Lillie was born in Belfast, New York, on September 23, 1856. Albert and Lillie settled into Princeton, where Albert's attention turned to the hotel his father built near the Princeton Depot. He gave the hotel the Knox name for the first time and managed it over the last nine years of his life. Albert and Lillie lived in the hotel for a while before taking residence on Elm Street, two blocks east of the hotel.

Albert passed on September 15, 1927, and was laid to rest in the family plot in Oakland Cemetery. Headstones were cut by A.C. Best, including one for Lillie. At Lillie's own passing in 1934, Oakland was not to be her resting place. She was returned to Belfast, New York, and buried with her brother and sister. At Albert's passing, Lillie served as the executrix for his sizable estate, which included the Knox Hotel and other properties. Unfortunately, the Benzant Gold Mining Company shares were of doubtful value.

Albert Knox, 1874.
Bureau County Historical Society, Princeton, Illinois
Immke Glass Plate Collection

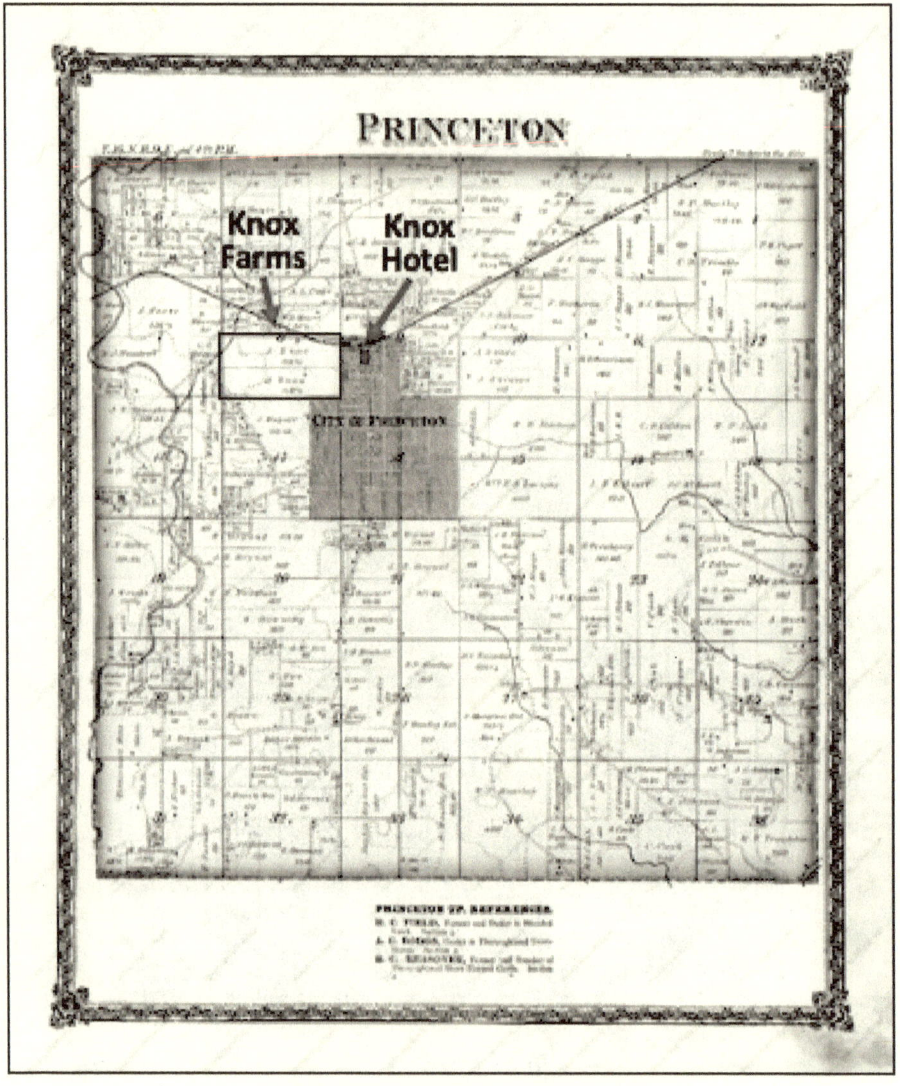

Princeton Township, Bureau County, Illinois, 1875
Copyrighted, Historic Map Works Online, LLC

GAR Medallion, Oakland Cemetery, Princeton, Illinois
Photo by Author, 2022

KNOX FAMILY TREE

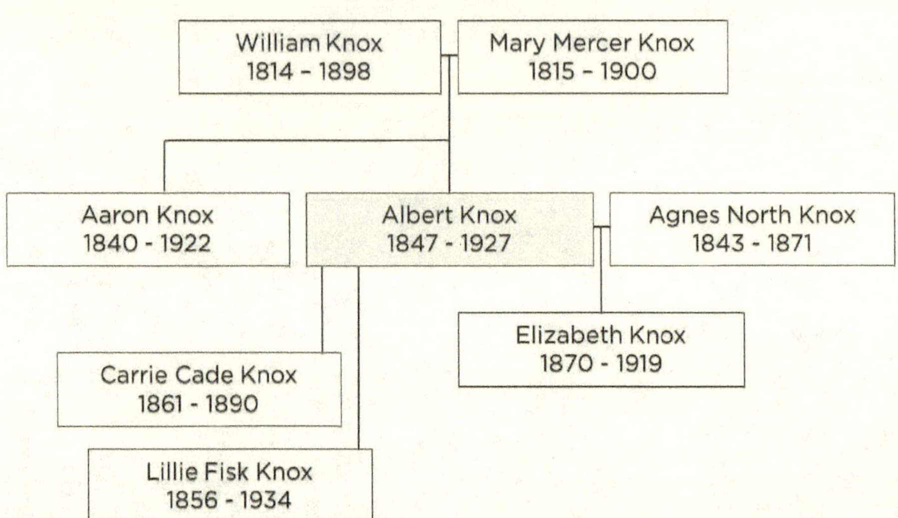

Samuel B. Hinsdale

George C. Hinsdale, one of the earliest settlers, arrived in Bureau County, Illinois, in 1831. The land was mostly virgin forest and prairie, and travel for both settlers and Native Americans was on long-established trails of the latter. Much of the Native American land was acquired through treaties, the terms of which often were ambiguous. Relationships among settlers and Native Americans reflected a long history of alliances and rivalries. Over time, Native Americans split loyalties between Britain and the United States. An example of split and shifting loyalties was seen in Chief Shabbona, one of the most known and respected of the Ottawa tribe. Shabbona had sided with the British in the War of 1812, but determined the better path forward was in alliance with the United States. An equally well known and respected chief was Black Hawk of the Sauk tribe. With the ceding of Native American land of the Old Northwest to the United States, most Native Americans resettled west of the Mississippi River. Black Hawk saw the treaty for Sauk land as unjust. With a large contingent, he crossed back over the Mississippi and the Black Hawk War of 1832 ensued. Shabbona played a notable role of providing advance warning to Bureau County settlers of potential attacks. Defeat resulted for the Native Americans in this, their last war east of the Mississippi.

Young people were encouraged to migrate from the east to take advantage of the fertile Illinois soil being sold cheaply. In Northampton, Massachusetts, a small group formed the Hampshire Colony Congregational Church on March 23, 1831. They determined to migrate west and settle in Illinois, the 21st state when admitted to the Union on December 3, 1818. Family and friends of this band of Christians were filled with foreboding for the risks ahead. They were true pioneers as *"the Indians, deer, prairie wolf and rattlesnakes held undisputed possession of all this land."*[13] The 1,000-mile journey from Northampton to Bureau County was arduous. The Hampshire Colonists departed May 7, 1831, and arrived at their final destination, the small settlement of Dover, Illinois, on July 4, 1831. They traveled overland westward from Northampton to Albany, New York, where they boarded a boat to traverse the 363 miles of the Erie Canal to Buffalo. A steamer transported them across Lake Erie to Detroit, Michigan. In Detroit, they hired teams to carry them to Chicago, and from Chicago on to Dover.

Samuel Dexter Hinsdale followed his older brother, George, to Bureau County in 1835. Their family home was in Greenfield, Massachusetts, twenty miles north of Northampton. The Hampshire Colonists chose a growing settlement south of Dover to establish the only Congregational Church in Illinois at that time. To honor their Massachusetts roots, the post office for the new settlement was named Greenfield. A lottery in 1833 changed Greenfield to Princeton, a name literally thrown into the hat by a settler from New Jersey. The incorporation of Princeton as a village would not transpire until 1838.

The Hampshire Colonists played a major role in the early development of Princeton. They set the priorities for the value of education and for moral standards, including strong and vocal support for abolition. Oakland Cemetery in Princeton was a gift of their church's first pastor, Lucian Farnham. He dedicated the land for the burial of his son in 1836. Owen Lovejoy migrated to Illinois from Maine in 1838. He was the second pastor at the Hampshire Colony Congregational Church. He was a staunch abolitionist, friend of Abraham Lincoln, member of the 35th U.S. Congress as a Republican Representative, and a "conductor" on the Underground Railroad. Religious faith and civic duty were strong traits of the settlers from New England, and these traits ran deep in the Hinsdale family.

George Hinsdale went straight to the business of farming and experienced early success, particularly with potatoes. Trading among settlers and remaining Native Americans continued at a brisk pace. Among the norms of the time was the trading of young Native American women. Daughters of tribal leaders were prime candidates for such trading. Young women would be traded with settlers as well for goods, food and livestock. George's abundant potato crop of 1832 drew the attention of local Native Americans, who proposed to swap a young maiden for some of his crop. He declined the offer. Both George and Samuel Dexter found marriages with daughters of early settlers.

Samuel Dexter's first wife was Jemima Carpenter, a native of New York State. Their marriage was blessed with six children. Their second born and first son was Samuel Burritt Hinsdale, born March 27, 1847. Early deaths for mothers and children were far too common at this time. Tragedy befell the Hinsdale family with the death of three children, one at age four and two at less than six months. Eight-year-old Burritt would lose his mother on July 4, 1855. His father, however, found commercial success as a pump dealer and a gunsmith. At his passing on December 20, 1875, he was eulogized as *"...genial and generous, and whole souled, and one everybody loved."*[14]

Samuel Dexter's real estate activity was modest. He held no agricultural land, and his development holdings were five lots in the Elston's Addition to Princeton. In current dollars, the total value of these lots was in excess of $300,000. However, he was active in personal lending, unrelated to real estate. At his passing, 36 loans were outstanding with an average current dollar value of $2,300.

Burritt answered the call of the Union Army and was mustered into Company A of the Illinois 139th Infantry Regiment on June 1, 1864, at Peoria, Illinois. The 139th was commissioned for a 100-day duty. Following pursuit of a guerrilla party, the Regiment was assigned to garrison duty at Cairo, Illinois. The next assignment was back to Peoria in anticipation of mustering out. However, St. Louis came under siege and President Lincoln himself ordered that the Regiment join its defense. Lincoln publicly thanked the troops for their extended duty and for their patriotism, a distinction that Burritt and his fellow soldiers valued. Burritt was mustered out of the 139th as a private in Peoria on October 28, 1864.

Burritt returned to civilian life in Princeton, but the 139th was not to be the end of his Union Army experience. A new Illinois Regiment, the 151st, was mustered in at Quincy, Illinois, on February 23, 1865. Burritt and his Regiment worked their way south to Dalton, Georgia, where the 151st was consolidated with three other Regiments, one each from Illinois, Indiana, and Ohio. The combination was now the First Brigade, Second Separate Division, Army of the Cumberland. They saw no fighting, but their mission was to receive the surrender of Confederate Army forces. They were to secure good order and guard government property. The 151st was mustered out at Columbus, Georgia, on January 24, 1866. Final discharge and payment were in Springfield, Illinois, on February 8, 1866. Burritt had risen to the rank of corporal. He was on his way back to civilian life for good, and he had some time between his tours of duty to contemplate life ahead. Burritt wasted no time and registered at the University of Notre Dame on March 21, 1866.

Fresh from his disciplined life as a soldier in the Union Army, Burritt embraced the structured student life at Notre Dame. He threw himself into all the university had to offer. By all measures, Burritt had an active, full experience at Notre Dame, both in the second semester of the 1865-1866 school year and in his return for the full 1866-1867 school year. At its annual commencement, Notre Dame conferred degrees and awarded premiums, the latter recognizing achievement in subjects across the whole of the academic fields and other attributes of importance. Generally, one premium was awarded per subject and one or more "accesserunts" (equivalent honorable mentions) received recognition. At the 22nd annual commencement held on June 27, 1866, Burritt was a four-time accesserunt: Senior Department Premium of Honor, Politeness, Neatness, and German. At the 23rd annual commencement held on June 26, 1867, his accesserunts grew to twelve. He repeated for Senior Department Premium of Honor, Politeness, Neatness, and German. To these were added Latin – Grammar & Theme, Vocal Music, Commercial Law, Bookkeeping Theory, Bookkeeping Execution, Bookkeeping Proficiency, Public Reading, and Calisthenics. He was an accomplished student who returned to Princeton, Illinois, well-prepared for his life journey ahead.

Burritt married Julia Elizabeth Nash, a Princeton native, on June 26, 1873. Born on October 13, 1849, Julia was the daughter of John E. and Charlotte Nash, natives of New York State. John was a dry goods merchant in Princeton and served the city in official capacities. He was marshal from 1865-1867 and truant ("humane") officer of the Princeton schools for many years. A resolution following his death in 1907 by the Board of Education noted that *"when it was found necessary to enforce the truant law, and with any fair-minded parent, he solved the problem without giving offense."*[15] Charlotte was a dressmaker, and she passed this talent on to Julia, who became a milliner. On the occasion of their 50th wedding anniversary in 1898, it was said of John and Charlotte that they *"are well and widely known for their excellent qualities of head and heart, being prominent workers for the uplifting of Princeton's moral and religious life."*[16]

Burritt was drawn to the opportunities in Chicago post the Great Fire of 1871. Chicago was a center for new technology of the day. He found his lifetime career in the field of court reporting and stenography, fields which were dominated at the time by male professionals. He was among the earliest stenographers in the country. Stenography, the use of rapid writing (shorthand), took on greater importance with the growth and needs of business and the professions, and stenograph machines were part of that technology wave. The first stenograph widely sold in the U.S. was invented by Miles Bartholomew, an Illinois court reporter, in 1877.

Burritt and Julia moved on to Woodbridge, New Jersey, in 1876. They were blessed with two daughters. Bertha was born February 7, 1877, and Edith Grace was born March 28, 1879. Burritt became a court reporter in New York City and the New Jersey counties of Middlesex and Monmouth. Over time, he established his own extensive court reporting business, employing many other professionals.

Burritt recorded a short, three-paragraph, last will and testament on May 2, 1886. The beneficiaries of all of his property, real and personal, were his beloved wife, Julia, and her heirs in succession. Following an illness of short duration, Burritt passed on December 27, 1903, at his Woodbridge home. He was laid to rest in the First Presbyterian churchyard, Middlesex County. Both his wife, Julia, and their daughter, Edith Grace Hinsdale, would join him there in 1919 and 1932, respectively.

Samuel Burritt Hinsdale, 1874.
Bureau County Historical Society, Princeton, Illinois
Immke Glass Plate Collection

Julia Nash Hinsdale, 1874.
Bureau County Historical Society, Princeton, Illinois
Immke Glass Plate Collection

Stenograph - Miles Bartholomew.
Patent #215,554. May 20, 1879.
Division of Work and Industry,
National Museum of American History, Smithsonian Institution

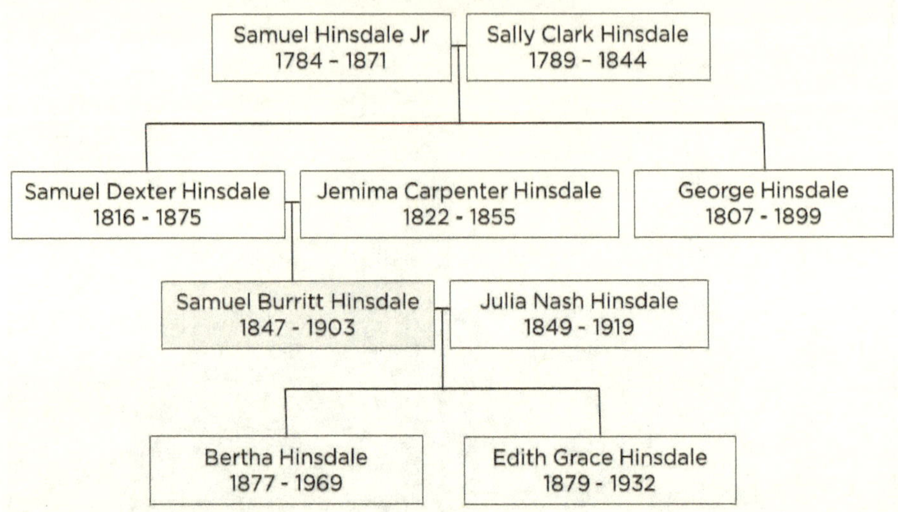
HINSDALE FAMILY TREE
Samuel Hinsdale Jr
1784 - 1871
Sally Clark Hinsdale
1789 - 1844
Samuel Dexter Hinsdale
1816 - 1875
Jemima Carpenter Hinsdale
1822 - 1855
George Hinsdale
1807 - 1899
Samuel Burritt Hinsdale
1847 - 1903
Julia Nash Hinsdale
1849 - 1919
Bertha Hinsdale
1877 - 1969
Edith Grace Hinsdale
1879 - 1932

Mark Templeton

"*Mark Templeton is dead. Thus, is ended the career of one of the well-known characters of Princeton, and for whom it can only be said: 'It might have been.'*"[17] Such was the judgmental reporting in the "Bureau County Republican" on December 23, 1897, of his passing seven days earlier. Mark A. Templeton was the fifth of eight young men from Princeton, Illinois, to attend the University of Notre Dame in the 1860s. Challenges befell him throughout a shortened, 48-year life that began with abandonment and was marked by loss.

Robert T. Templeton and Leonora Weise were married in Princeton, Illinois, on June 4, 1846. Born October 20, 1811, in Chambersburg, Pennsylvania, Robert got a leg up on his business career when the interest in his uncle William's mercantile business was transferred to him in 1842. A Princeton business directory of 1845 listed him as a dealer in dry goods, groceries and queensware. He was drawn to government positions and occupied several during his life. He was the Bureau County treasurer in both 1837 and 1839. He was one of 20 qualified voters who cast ballots in March 1838, unanimously incorporating the village of Princeton. He was elected to the first town council in 1857 and served as council president in all but one year from 1859 to 1864. He became Judge of the Bureau County Court in December 1849 and was so referenced as Judge Templeton thereafter. He was a member of the Illinois State Constitutional Convention of 1862. Judge Templeton was a prolific investor in land and real estate as well.

Leonora Weise was one of nine children born to Jacob and Mary

Weise. She was born July 11, 1824, in Morris County, New Jersey. Her family migrated to Princeton where Jacob was a successful real estate investor, including land that eventually became a sizable portion of the town's northeast development. Her parents spent the remainder of their lives in Princeton, as did Leonora and four of her siblings.

In the mid-1800s, the number of orphaned or abandoned children in major cities of the eastern United States grew along with rising urban populations and increasingly crowded conditions. Many such children were born to immigrant, laborer parents. The more fortunate children were sheltered in foundling homes, although governmental regulation and oversight were limited. The first statewide adoption act was passed by Massachusetts in 1851. The less fortunate were left to homeless lives, where protection from violence often could be found in the company of street gangs.

Well-intended concerned citizens saw an opportunity for placing orphans in the newly-opening midwestern and western territories. Rapidly-expanding and labor-intensive agricultural communities required more hands, and children of the cities could help fill the worker shortage. One solution was the so-called "orphan trains," supervised although unregulated welfare programs with overtones of evangelical humanitarianism. An example of a more structured program was one conducted by the "New England Home for Little Wanderers," working through local clergy at identified towns on rail lines. Trains with children arrived on Saturday, and a discussion of duty, purpose, and care took place in churches on Sunday with both orphan children and prospective parents in attendance. Adoptions were completed on Monday. Less humane were programs in which families interested in adoption showed up at local train stations where newly-arrived orphans were placed on display. Placements often were made with little scrutiny of prospective parents or consent of the child.

Mark Templeton was born in 1849 and was placed in a foundling home in the eastern United States. By 1855, he was listed in the Illinois State Census as a resident in the Princeton home of Robert and Leonora Templeton. The Templetons were well-established and well-regarded in the community. Mark joined a family of means with a patriarch whose accomplishments set a very high bar.

Mark lost his only-child distinction in the family when Leonora gave birth to a daughter, Mary Ross Templeton, in 1862. Mary's birth was a cause for special celebration, with Robert in his 50s and Leonora approaching 40. As they were her birth parents, Mary enjoyed a biological parent-child relationship not possible for Mark. Two cousins of Robert held special places in the family. Cousin Mary Ross Templeton Hewetson was the namesake of Robert and Leonora's daughter. Cousin James Wilson Templeton was accomplished in his own right in Princeton, Bureau County, and Illinois. The cousins were children of Robert's uncle William, who earlier helped further Robert's business career.

Only three years following daughter Mary's birth, Judge Robert Templeton passed on February 4, 1865. Days earlier, on January 24, he had recorded his last will and testament. He left an estate valued in excess of five million current dollars.

Robert Templeton was one of the largest individual landowners in Bureau County. At his passing, his agricultural land holdings were just shy of 1,300 acres, with a value in current dollars in excess of $5.5 million. He was a prolific lender as well, with 116 loans outstanding with a total current dollar value approaching $1.2 million. With loans at 21% of his real estate portfolio value, he was a moderate risk-taker. Fortunately, the majority of his loans were listed as "good." Approximately one-third of his loans were listed as "doubtful" or "desperate." Robert provided a substantial legacy for his widow, daughter and adopted son.

The County Court of Bureau County, Illinois, was petitioned on February 9, 1865, for the probate of Robert T. Templeton's will and letters testamentary. The documents were voluminous. Joseph I. Taylor and Andrew Weise (brother of Leonora) were appointed executors. After first providing for his debts and funeral expenses, Robert directed simple bequests to one sister and three nephews.

He next provided for his *"beloved wife Leonora Templeton"*[18] and his *"infant child Mary Ross Templeton."*[19] In addition to the homestead and personal property, they were to be supported by the rental income from the "Fountain Farm" that he owned. The farm was occupied under a lease to Andrew Weise. Taylor was given sole power to determine terms of the lease renewal and future settlements. Support and maintenance for Mary was specified only until she attained the age of 13 years. However, the terms for Mark, age 16 at the time, were most explicit and extensive.

"I commit to the care, custody, control and direction of my wife, my adopted son Mark Templeton, until he shall attain the age of his majority, and it is my desire that she secure to him (if practicable) a good English education and to that end it is my will and desire that the Trustees hereinafter appointed shall from time to time as may be required, pay over to my said wife such sum or sums of money, out of the proceeds of my estate, as they, the said Trustees, and my said wife shall deem necessary for the expenses and costs incident to his procuring such education. And it is further my will and desire that if the said Mark Templeton shall continue to abide with my said wife or elsewhere under her direction, until he shall attain the age of twenty one years, and shall during all this time of his minority betake himself to habits of industry, economy and prudence and shall during the same time render a respectful obedience to the reasonable commands of my said wife that then (the said Trustees and my said wife concurring in judgment that the said Mark so lived and demeaned himself) the said Trustees shall be required to pay over to the said Mark Templeton out of the money then in their hands belonging to my estate the sum of two thousand dollars."[20]

Notre Dame grew through and after the Civil War. In the 1867-1868 school year, 448 students enrolled, 23% more than enrolled with Lewis Thompson in 1863. Students represented 26 of 37 states, one territory (Montana), the District of Columbia, and one foreign country, Ireland. The student home-state profile changed materially in four years, reflecting in part the resolution and impact of the War.

Students from the former Confederate states fell by 50%, an understandable outcome given the loss of life and assets, and the recovery that progressed slowly. On the other hand, notable growth in enrollment came from states experiencing growth and development from the continuing westward migration. Such states included Missouri, Iowa, Kentucky, and Colorado. Illinois surpassed Indiana with most enrolled students, reflecting in part the rapid growth and prosperity of Chicago.

Notre Dame expanded its capabilities to support the growing enrollment. In four years, faculty increased 45% to 48, resulting in an appealing student to faculty ratio of 9:1. Perhaps most notable, Notre Dame provided this quality education at an all-in cost that had declined by 30% over four years. To be sure, a college education in 1867 of this nature was beyond the financial means of most Americans.

Whether a loving father-figure or a stern taskmaster, Robert was arguably the most important male in Mark's life at a time when important decisions would be made for his life path. With Robert's passing, Mark lost the voice of guidance and direction, as well as patronage to the local community and beyond. Leonora stepped in and fulfilled Robert's wish for Mark's education. Mark arrived at the University of Notre Dame on February 4, 1868, to attend the second half of the 1867-1868 school year.

Notre Dame prided itself on the disciplined environment it maintained. They stated in the Annual Catalogue for the 1867-1868 school year that discipline *"...is mild, yet sufficiently energetic to preserve the most perfect order and regularity. The morals and the general deportment of the Pupils are assiduously watched over, and their comforts and personal habits receive the same attention as if they were in the bosom of their own families."*[21] Among the enforced regulations were silence except during times of recreation, no use of tobacco, and the prohibition of intoxicating liquors.

Mark adapted to this environment and he returned on September 1, 1868, for the 1868-1869 school year. Notre Dame recorded in its daybook the cash payments from Leonora for

Mark's college education. Surviving records contain no details regarding Mark's school activities or academic pursuits. If, as with his predecessors, he enrolled in Notre Dame's Commercial Course, classes included arithmetic, English, bookkeeping, German, geography, and history. Open to him as well were optional studies in Spanish, Italian, Hebrew, painting, drawing, and music. It was an environment in which a motivated individual could thrive and a less disciplined student could be overwhelmed.

Mark returned to Princeton and took up residence again with his mother and sister. 1872 found him drawn to the opportunities provided by the frenetic recovery and rebuilding of Chicago from the Great Fire, and he gained employment as a carpenter. His boarding residence was on the same Cottage Grove Avenue as the Jacob Fetrow residence.

In 1878, double loss befell the Templeton family. Leonora Templeton suffered a stroke. Soon thereafter, Mary Ross Templeton died of diphtheria at age 15. Within a year, tragedy struck Leonora again. A second stroke left her paralyzed and voiceless. She spent the last four years of her life as if *"buried in a living tomb."*[22] By 1880, Mark again was residing in the Princeton family home, with Leonora and a housekeeper, Sarah Templeton. For the first time in a U.S. Census, he was recorded as a son, albeit adopted.

Leonora died on May 19, 1883. She left no will for an estate valued in excess of four million current dollars. The initial court filing of her estate on June 2, 1883, stated that she left no husband or child, even though her adopted son, Mark, clearly survived her. The beneficiaries of her estate were her own surviving siblings, two brothers and four sisters. There was no provision for Mark. This was a significant exclusion, and one with no stated explanation. However, the stage had been set for such an outcome in Robert's last will and testament of 18 years earlier. Mark was dealt a double loss, to his sense of family belonging and acceptance and to his future financial well-being.

Claims against Leonora's estate were revealing. Sarah Templeton was more than a housekeeper. She was Robert's niece.

In 1870, she came to live with the family and be in service to them. Following Leonora's paralysis, Sarah took on additional duties as her fulltime caregiver. Sarah filed a detailed claim seeking back wages from the very beginning of her service. She carefully offset the value of gifts she had received and as well as her wages for an eight-week leave. The estate executors concurred with her claim and the court approved payment in full. Delano & Son was one of Princeton's oldest and well-regarded grocers. The proprietor submitted a claim to Leonora's estate for produce delivered as far back as three years prior to her death. This claim was honored as well.

The management of Templeton family affairs slid into disarray after Robert's passing, even while Leonora remained of sound mind and body. No one, including Mark, provided oversight or control. In providing for Mark as he did in his will, Robert's earlier concern for Mark's life path appeared prophetic. Robert, Leonora and Mary Ross all were gone, and with them emotional support. So long as financial support was forthcoming from Leonora, he lacked incentive for steady employment. Without a skilled trade or profession, his financial future darkened. Mark had developed a propensity for alcohol at an early age. Alcoholism now tightened its grip on him.

The theory of medicine and the practice of medical treatment traced a steady line of progression over millennia, and the second half of the 1800s was no exception. Change often arose in response to societal needs. Treating victims of war, particularly on the scale of Civil War casualties and the lessons learned therein, was strong impetus. Deeply embedded practices, however, often were slow to change even in light of valid new evidence or experience. An example was bloodletting, which continued well into the 1900s. The history of treating alcoholism took a particular direction in the late 1800s that reflected other societal issues as much as advances in medical science themselves.

Mark's alcoholism was notable enough in the community that the Women's Club of Princeton identified him as one for whom special care should be provided. On December 16, 1893, he was among a group of men sent to the Keeley Institute in Dwight, Illinois, to take the Keeley Cure. Leslie Keeley was a graduate of the respected Rush Medical College in Chicago and had served as a surgeon in the Union Army. He believed that alcoholism was a disease that he could cure. The treatment, first announced in 1879, had gained national popularity at the time of Mark's arrival. It consisted first of letting patients drink as much alcohol as they could imbibe, and then they were subjected to injections of bichloride of gold, the "gold cure," four times daily for four weeks. There were other tonics given as well. The cure did not "take" for Mark, and he returned to Princeton in precarious physical and financial conditions. Long after his death in 1900, Leslie Keeley was labeled as *"a common, ordinary quack with a useless remedy which made good by advertising and catching suckers."*[22]

Mark's fortunes declined further, and his activities in Princeton became the subject of gossip-oriented, disparaging commentary in the local press. He was referred to as Mark Temp. Before his travel to the Keeley Institute, he was called *"a sot and nuisance."*[23] Two years later, it was said he *"was made a tool of by others in formulating a complaint"*[24] against a local businessman. The intended victim *"retaliated upon the luckless and shiftless Mark by laying in a charge of vagrancy against him."*[25] Mark was arrested and spent four months in jail.

As county judge, Robert Templeton would have been well aware of the county almshouse or poorhouse, generally known as the County Farm. In 1852, Bureau County commissioners passed a resolution appropriating $1,000 to establish a poor farm and ordered the purchase of 160 acres west of Princeton for the County Farm. An 1881 report to the Illinois General Assembly on county almshouses indicated that the Bureau County Farm was worthy of high praise. The County required all paupers who were supported entirely by County expense to go to the County Farm. The earliest daybooks for the farm, titled "Poor House Register," revealed that poverty was not the only attribute of inmates. Indicative of societal norms of the time, inmates were registered with "diseases" including "insane," "imbecile," "idiotic," "defective speech," "homeless," and "cripple."

For several of his last winters, Mark was an inmate of the Bureau County Farm. The annual report of the County Farm Committee, dated September 1898, listed ten deaths in the reporting period. They ranged in age from 26 days to 77 years. Mark was one of the ten, dying there on December 16, 1897, at age 48. He succumbed to chronic ulceration of the stomach, an affliction often associated with alcoholism. He was laid to rest in the county burying grounds on the Farm property, where the remains of other inmates were interred in unmarked graves. The bookends of Mark A. Templeton's life were institutions to which society turned for the abandoned.

Robert T. Templeton, 1860s.
Bureau County Historical Society, Princeton, Illinois
Immke Glass Plate Collection

Mary Ross Templeton, 1862-1863.
Bureau County Historical Society, Princeton, Illinois
Immke Glass Plate Collection

The Keeley Institute
Taking the Hypodermic Treatment, 1893
Courtesy of the University of Illinois

Bureau County Farm Cemetery
Bureau County, Illinois
Photo by Author, 2023

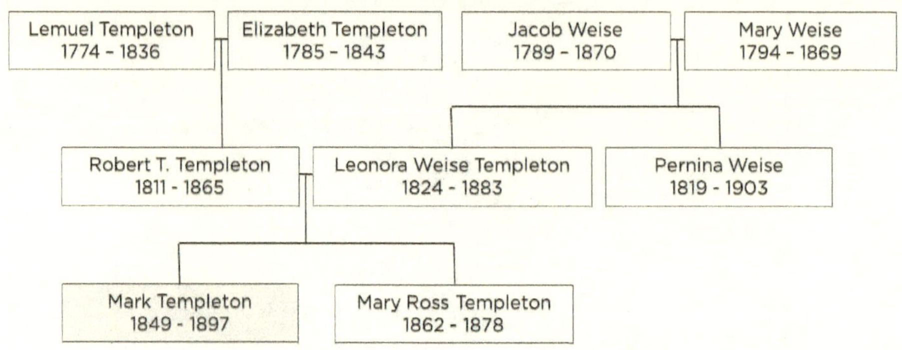
TEMPLETON FAMILY TREE
Lemuel Templeton
1774 - 1836
Elizabeth Templeton
1785 - 1843
Jacob Weise
1789 - 1870
Mary Weise
1794 - 1869
Robert T. Templeton
1811 - 1865
Leonora Weise Templeton
1824 - 1883
Pernina Weise
1819 - 1903
Mark Templeton
1849 - 1897
Mary Ross Templeton
1862 - 1878

John L. Dodge

John L. Dodge experienced a lot of living in his early years. He was born on June 6, 1855, in Princeton, Illinois. He was the third son and fifth of six children born to John Dodge and Hannah Crownover Dodge. His father was a native of New York State, and his mother was born in Pennsylvania. John L. was too young for the Civil War draft to touch him, but he was old enough to see and take note of the impact on other families in his community. He was free to enjoy all that bucolic Bureau County had to offer – hiking Native American paths; swimming and fishing in big Bureau Creek; observing the challenges and accomplishments of farm life through his friends and their families. But John L.'s idealistic youth was overshadowed by early and significant life tragedies. He lost his younger brother and closest sibling, George. George was the youngest of the Dodge children, and he passed on January 18, 1862, at age 4. This loss took a toll on all the family, but none more so than mother Hannah. Six years later, Hannah died unexpectedly on January 11, 1868, at age 40. Her loss opened a hole in John L.'s life that never would be filled.

From its founding in 1842 to well into the 20th Century, Notre Dame maintained a separate program for preparatory education. It was known as the Minim Department and its inmates were boys ages 6 to 13. The "Minims" had separate rooms and recreation yards. They were taught by the Sisters of the Holy Cross, who oversaw their care, including clothing and personal hygiene. They were instructed in all the elementary branches of an English education, including spelling, reading, writing, English grammar, geography, history, and arithmetic. Added to these courses were basic Latin, French, and German. Their school days had no less than six hours of study but never more than two successive hours in the classroom. Students completing the Minim program were found to be better prepared for the next level of education than those from a general education background. Fr. Edward Sorin, the founder of Notre Dame, supported the Minim program from the beginning and gave them special recognition as the "Princes" of the University. Among the Minims were the son of General William Sherman, the son of Knute Rockne, and John L. Dodge.

On February 11, 1868, one week after the arrival on campus of Mark Templeton, John L. was registered at Notre Dame. While listed at age 10 in the Notre Dame daybook, he was in fact 12, but nonetheless eligible for admission to the Minim Department.

John L. found an environment at Notre Dame much different from any he experienced at home. His father was replaced by the nuns and his siblings by many young boys of various backgrounds and upbringings. It was an environment of discipline with a rigid schedule:

6:30AM - arise, toilet, etc.

7:00AM - breakfast, exercise

7:30AM - study

9:30AM - lunch, recreation

10:00AM - study

11:45AM - toilet

12:00PM - dinner, recreation

1:30PM - study

3:30PM - lunch, recreation

6:30PM - supper, recreation

8:30PM - retire

Baths were taken every Saturday, and underclothing was changed regularly twice a week. *"The greatest care is taken to form their young hearts to habits of virtue, and to inculcate the practice of refined manners. Every effort is made to foster respect and affection for parents, to whom they are expected to write once a week."*[26]

John L.'s experience was determined of such benefit to his development that he would continue his Notre Dame education. He returned for the next school year running from September 1, 1868, to June 23, 1869, but not alone. Returning with him was his older brother, Hiram, who at age 18 enrolled in the Senior Department of Notre Dame.

The brothers Dodge returned to Princeton following their year together at Notre Dame. Their father was advanced in years, but of sound mind and memory, and would record his last will and testament on September 11, 1871. John Dodge passed within a month on October 8, 1871. He left a sizable estate to be administered by two executors, one of whom was his brother-in-law, James Crownover.

John's real estate holdings were substantial, and, like Robert Templeton, he was a profuse lender. At his passing, his agricultural land holdings were well in excess of 500 acres. His development land holdings included 12 lots in three different towns. The value of all his real estate was in excess of $3.1 million current dollars. He had extended 80 loans with a total current dollar value in excess of $3.0 million. With loans at 97% of his real estate portfolio value, he was a risk-taker. Fortunately, very few of his loans were listed as less than "good."

John's will directed that his estate be divided roughly equally among his five surviving children, but his first provision was for John L., his youngest surviving child. As a minor, John L.'s bequest was to be held in trust for his benefit until reaching age 21, five years hence. The trust was under the direction of the same estate executors.

The stalwart of the Dodge siblings was the oldest, Elizabeth ("Libbie"), born July 16, 1846. She married a Civil War veteran and surgeon, Owen Jason Evans. Evans served a full three years in the Union Army with the 40th Infantry of New York. He mustered out after the war's end. They relocated to Minneapolis, where Dr. Evans was active both in his own practice and in the local medical community. He served on the advisory board of the Minnesota Medical Hospital in its early years along with other notable figures of the Minneapolis community, including several members of the prominent Pillsbury family. With their financial well-being established, Libbie reached out to assist her siblings. At age 14, John L. moved to Minneapolis to live with his older sister after completing his studies at Notre Dame.

The estate of John Dodge remained open for almost five years. John L. felt the time had come to change who controlled his life, and he petitioned the Bureau County Court on October 19, 1874, to appoint his older brother, Jay, as his legal guardian. Jay was the firstborn son and six years senior to John L. While two years remained until age 21 and gaining full control of his inheritance, John L. preferred living under the direction of his brother. The Court approved and Jay accepted this guardianship role the same day it was petitioned. Jay was to have care of and custody and management of property for the education and support of his younger brother.

A report sometime later and a distance removed from Bureau County cast events in a somewhat different light. John L. was reported to have visited Tampico, Illinois, in late 1884 on matters related to his wealthy father's estate. However, the estate had been settled and closed in 1876. It was further reported that John L. left Tampico with a "borrowed" overcoat and an unpaid hotel bill. The reporter concluded that this was, *"another illustration of the old, old story of inherited wealth falling into hands too weak to hold it …"*[27] John Dodge's instinct of protecting his son's financial future was well-intended but subverted in the end.

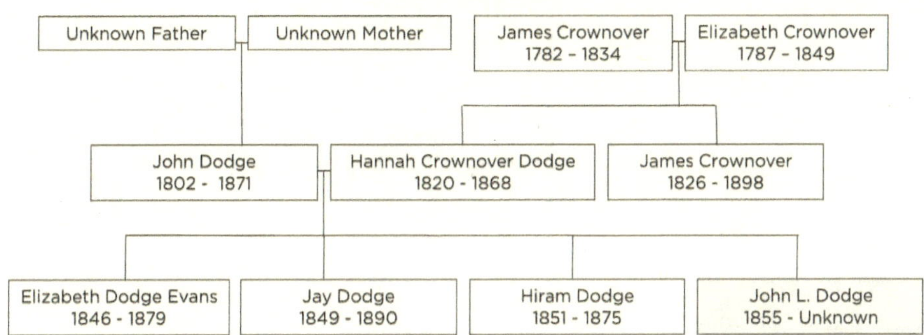
DODGE FAMILY TREE
Unknown Father
Unknown Mother
James Crownover 1782 - 1834
Elizabeth Crownover 1787 - 1849
John Dodge 1802 - 1871
Hannah Crownover Dodge 1820 - 1868
James Crownover 1826 - 1898
Elizabeth Dodge Evans 1846 - 1879
Jay Dodge 1849 - 1890
Hiram Dodge 1851 - 1875
John L. Dodge 1855 - Unknown

Hiram Dodge

Hiram Dodge was born in Princeton, Illinois, on January 12, 1851, the second son and third of six children born to John Dodge and Hannah Crownover Dodge. Hiram attended the University of Notre Dame from September 1, 1868, to June 23, 1869. He was to benefit from the educational experience, but he also was to look out for his younger brother.

The Panic of 1873 took a toll on the global economy. For the U.S., the post-Civil War boom turned to a multi-year bust. Inflation rose along with unemployment. Bankruptcies cascaded through the country's growth industry, railroads. No part of the U.S. was untouched, and job opportunities dwindled, even for a young man such as Hiram with an advanced education.

Hiram never married, and he traveled away from Princeton in pursuit of opportunities. In his teenage years, he developed his skill as a harness maker. Travel took him to Iowa, Minnesota, and Pennsylvania. His sister, Libbie, took him into her Minneapolis home, where he stayed for an extended period. She financed his travel to Williamsport, Pennsylvania, as well. Hiram was the last child to be provided for in his father's 1871 will. The terms of the provision indicated a level of concern over Hiram's financial responsibility. Whereas his younger siblings, Genevieve and John L., would have funds in trust released to them at age 21, Hiram was to receive only interest and income from his trust until age 30.

Unfortunately, Hiram did not reach this milestone, as he died in Williamsport well before his 30th birthday, on July 19, 1875. Unfortunately, sister Libbie outlived Hiram by a mere four years, passing at age 31 on January 23, 1879. She fought for the last year of her life against consumption, i.e., tuberculosis. Libbie received the best care possible, as her husband, O. J. Evans, was a noted physician. Hiram had a propensity to live beyond his means. He borrowed from some and traded on credit with others. Many came forward in the probate of his estate to make their claims. Among the claimants was his own brother-in-law, Dr. Evans. Dr. Evans and Libbie provided for Hiram's housing without compensation for over a year. They extended cash advances to him as well as covered some of his debts. Their total claim was in excess of $34,000 current dollars. Notable as well was a claim by a clothier and tailor for an extensive list of finery. All claims were paid by the estate's executor, Hiram's uncle James Crownover. Hiram died with one piece of real property, a two-year-old colt.

Hiram Dodge was laid to rest with his parents in Princeton's Oakland Cemetery.

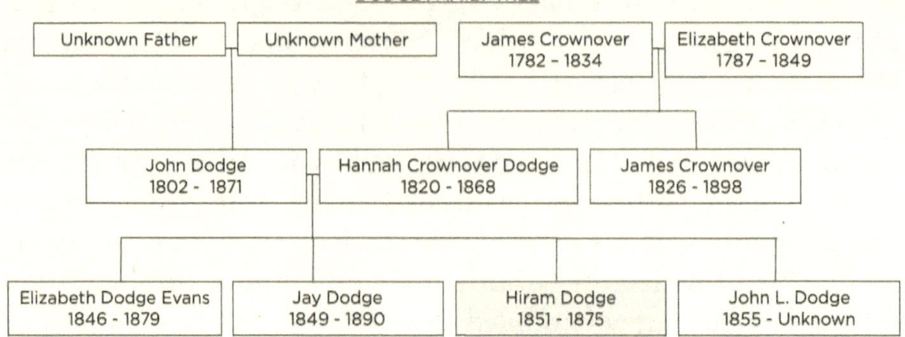
DODGE FAMILY TREE
Unknown Father
Unknown Mother
James Crownover 1782 - 1834
Elizabeth Crownover 1787 - 1849
John Dodge 1802 - 1871
Hannah Crownover Dodge 1820 - 1868
James Crownover 1826 - 1898
Elizabeth Dodge Evans 1846 - 1879
Jay Dodge 1849 - 1890
Hiram Dodge 1851 - 1875
John L. Dodge 1855 - Unknown

Franklin Pierce Thomson

Franklin Pierce was the 14th president of the United States and served one term, 1853-1857. He was a New England Democrat, chosen as a compromise candidate who could bridge Northern and Southern interests. He was seen as an honest man of conviction but lacking in decision-making skills. This shortcoming led to instability and opened the door for the U.S. Congress to play a more dominant role in setting policy. Like Abraham Lincoln after him, Pierce was a nationalist, intent on keeping the Union together. But Pierce publicly opposed Lincoln and entry into the Civil War. His personal life was highlighted by tragedy in the deaths of all three children at young ages. Excessive drinking continued through his life and was the proximate cause of his death. Franklin Pierce's name, however, lived on in one of the students who found his way to the University of Notre Dame in the mid-19th century.

Jacob Theodore Thomson was born November 2, 1812, in Changewater, New Jersey, to a family that valued education. He came to Princeton, Illinois, in 1846. He was successful in the general merchandise trade. He was successful as well in real estate investing. He acquired land far removed from Bureau County, but his largest holdings were in Princeton township and Princeton proper. Jacob partnered with his friends Milo Kendall and Joseph Thompson (father of Lewis Thompson) on tracts of land that would be developed into a large section of Princeton's northeast quadrant.

Jacob was particularly active in lending, both secured and unsecured, to his fellow citizens of Princeton. Such lending was relatively common from individuals of means and not driven by altruism. Particularly in small communities, people knew each other quite well. A shrewd lender could discern the creditworthiness of his borrowers. Terms of maturity were not long and 10% rates of interest provided attractive returns. Loans secured by fairly-valued collateral were preferred. The land development of Thomson, Kendall, and Thompson within Princeton was named the Union Addition. Jacob extended credit to many buyers of lots in this development. If buyers defaulted and new loans were not forthcoming, the developers merely got their land back plus whatever funds had been paid to date.

Jacob served more than one term as mayor of Princeton. With respect to his own political views, it was said, *"Strong and positive in his democracy, his party fealty was not grounded on partisan prejudice, and he enjoyed the respect and confidence of all his associates irrespective of party."*[28] He had much in common with Franklin Pierce.

Jacob married twice to sisters. His first wife, Mary Weise, died November 23, 1851, at age 30. Not interested in living alone, Jacob did not look far for a second wife, as he married Mary's sister, Pernina. Mary and Pernina were sisters of Leonora Weise, adoptive mother of Mark Templeton. Four children came of the marriage of Jacob and Pernina, the second of whom was a boy born October 25, 1852. They named him Franklin Pierce Thomson. This was a patriotic gesture reflecting the recent election of President Franklin Pierce. As the President's own fortunes waned, Franklin Pierce Thomson found carrying his full name uncomfortable. In his last will and testament recorded July 4, 1872, his own father referred to him as Frank P. Throughout his adult life, he was known as Frank P. Thomson.

Frank was the last of eight students from Princeton to attend the University of Notre Dame in the 1860s. He was well aware of the university before his arrival. He knew of all his predecessors and benefited from the perspectives and experiences of the first student, Lewis Thompson (son of his own father's business partner) and his cousin, Mark Templeton. In fact, Frank was not alone on his journey from Princeton to Notre Dame for the school year running from September 1, 1868, to June 23, 1869. He was in the company of cousin Mark and the Dodge brothers, John L. and Hiram. At age 15, Frank enrolled in the Commercial Course as did other students from Princeton before him. Notre Dame allowed parents to deposit money with the University that could be drawn on by their student for personal reasons. While most students did not have such an account, Frank benefited from a 50¢ per week stipend. This was meaningful spending money, as all other expenses were covered. In comparison, Hiram and John L. were allowed 15¢ and 10¢ respectively. Mark had no such provision.

Notre Dame changed much in the decade of the 1860s. Enrollment rose from 198 to 439, with a high of 505 in 1865. Quality of education rose as well, with expanded fields of study. Faculty increased from 14 to 38, reducing the student/faculty ratio from 14.1 to 11.6. Significant additions of buildings on campus were made over the decade. Tuition, room and board increased from $135 in 1860 to $150 in 1869, an increase of only +1.1% per year. Throughout the decade, students came from 25 states (of the 37 as of 1869), 3 territories, the District of Columbia and 5 foreign countries. Students found a rich education at Notre Dame, both in and out of the classroom.

There was much for Frank to do with his father's extensive business and land interests and activities. Frank married Mary J. Baumbaugh, a fellow Princeton native, and settled into the life of the city. They were blessed with one daughter, Pernina ("Nina") Cordelia Thomson, born January 17, 1884.

Jacob's real estate holdings were extensive and expansive, including more than 1,400 acres and 13 lots owned outright. While much of the property he owned was in Bureau County, he held land and lots elsewhere, including Chicago and LaSalle in Illinois, Lincoln in Nebraska, and Tarrant County and the town of Denton in Texas. The value in current dollars was in excess of $4.7 million. Jacob was a more modest lender relative to his landowner peers. At his passing, 41 loans were outstanding, equaling in value only 7% of his holdings. Most of these loans were within a partnership in which he was a one-third owner. The borrowers were individuals purchasing lots in the Union Addition to Princeton.

In the terms of his final will and testament as recorded February 16, 1876, Jacob Thomson designated one third of his estate to his wife, Pernina. The balance was to be split equally among his four surviving children. While Frank had reached the age of majority, Jacob determined that a portion of Frank's bequest was to be held in trust until he reached age 25 for good reason. Jacob passed six days later on February 22.

Jacob left a sizable estate and specific directions that properties outside of Princeton were to be sold in an expeditious manner. While the executors attempted to do so, Jacob's estate remained open over 17 years. Throughout this time, however, Pernina and her children received regular payouts sufficient to support comfortable lifestyles. Frank did not lack financial means, but a past of financial excess was revealed in the probate process. Unlike his father, the lender, Frank was a prolific borrower. Claims came early to Jacob's estate from creditors of Frank. One such claim from another prominent Princeton resident, Henry Wingert, was granted status as a direct recipient of a portion of Frank's estate distributions throughout the life of the estate.

Franklin Pierce ("Frank P.") Thomson passed on August 12, 1884. He had signed his last will and testament one year earlier, on August 7, 1883. At the age of 31, he left his widow Mary and eight-month-old daughter Nina to carry on. Once again, Jacob's sizable estate came to the rescue. Payments designated for Frank flowed through to Mary, permitting her to move forward with support for mother and daughter. All was not lost.

Jacob T. Thomson, 1876
Bureau County Historical Society, Princeton, Illinois
Immke Glass Plate Collection

Franklin Pierce Thomson, 1876
Bureau County Historical Society, Princeton, Illinois
Immke Glass Plate Collection

THOMSON FAMILY TREE

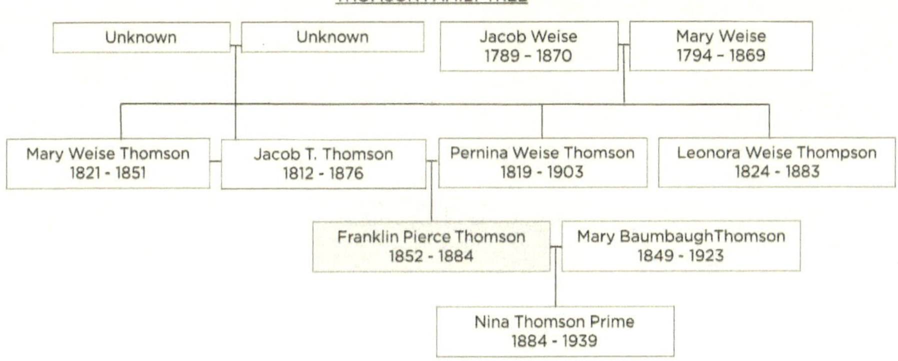

Connections

Events both in the U.S. (the War of 1812) and in Europe (the Napoleonic Wars of 1803 – 1815) brought conflict, disruption, displacement, and changing fortunes and opportunities. The result was a significant migration from Europe to and across the expanding U.S. In the Treaty of Paris of 1783, the region known as the Old Northwest was ceded to the United States. The territory encompassed six future U.S. states including Indiana (1816) and Illinois (1818).

Fr. Edward J. Sorin, CSC, was born on February 6, 1814, in Ahuillé, France. He was ordained a Roman Catholic priest on May 27, 1838. In 1839, he joined a relatively new order, the Congregation of the Holy Cross. In 1841, Sorin was sent to Indiana along with six Holy Cross brothers to establish a mission. They arrived at an outpost near the south branch of the St. Joseph River in November 1842. Sorin wasted no time, and in 1843 the state of Indiana issued a charter for the University of Notre Dame du Lac. In addition to being its founder, Sorin would serve as its first president over 21 years. He was the driving force taking Notre Dame from a vision to an ever-expanding reality throughout the 1800s. He was active in university affairs up to his death on October 31, 1893.

Andrew Gosse was born on April 28, 1812. With his parents, he emigrated from Eschweiler, Alsace, Germany, disembarking at the port of New York in 1831. He then traveled directly to Detroit, Michigan, where his father died. In 1839, Gosse and a group of contemporaries relocated to Bureau County, Illinois. Andrew married Eva Wiltz, a native of Bavaria, Germany, on June 6,

1843. Ten children were born to Eva and Andrew. Andrew took up brickmaking in Princeton, Illinois, and built the business to a sizable scale, manufacturing over one million bricks a year for several years. At one time, his was the only brickyard in Bureau County. Andrew also was engaged in farming, owning one of the largest farms in Princeton township. He was active as well in other commercial and residential real estate endeavors in Princeton. Andrew and Eva were Catholics, a minority in Princeton, which was heavily populated by Protestant Christians. They donated land for building the first Catholic church in Princeton. Andrew died on January 2, 1890.

Joseph V. Thompson was born in England on October 31, 1814. He was a native of Lancashire. His father died when Joseph was 12, and he began working as a shoemaker. By 1834, he had his own shop and employed several journeymen. He married Mary Kent in 1835. They migrated to the U.S. in 1837, settling in Genesee County, New York, and engaged in farming. In 1839, they journeyed to Toledo, Ohio, via canal, and on to Bureau County by wagon. Joseph continued farming and over time acquired a large tract in Walnut Township. Two sons were born to Mary and Joseph, Lewis and George. When Mary died on September 15, 1847, at age 37, George was sent back to Genesee County to be raised by his aunt. Joseph remarried and in time moved into Princeton. He occupied civic positions and engaged in real estate activities including the partnership with Jacob Thomson and Milo Kendall that developed the city's Union addition. Joseph passed on May 13, 1871.

These contemporaries, Edward Sorin, Andrew Gosse, and Joseph Thompson, natives of France, Germany and England respectively, would become connected in the Old Northwest of the U.S.

Through advertisements and his connections with Catholic priests, Andrew was well aware of Notre Dame. Interest extended to his own children. With support from Andrew and Eva, son Jacob Gosse corresponded to the university in 1870, showing a strong interest in admission. He knew of the eight students who attended Notre Dame in the 1860s. His career interest in pharmacy, however, took his education in a different direction. His youngest sister, Eva, attended St. Mary's, Notre Dame's companion college for women. Eva was musically inclined, but her avocation was oversight of the family businesses over much of her life.

Although a Protestant Christian, Joseph was aware of Notre Dame and his business and civic connections with Andrew provided a trusted consultant for the future education of his first-born son, Lewis Thompson. Lewis' admission and attendance at Notre Dame in 1863 brought the Thompsons in direct contact with Fr. Sorin, as he reviewed and approved all admissions. The circle of the connectedness among Edward, Andrew, and Joseph was complete, launching Notre Dame educations for eight young men from Princeton over eight consecutive years. While many other Princeton youth have attended Notre Dame in the decades since, no similar record of consecutive attendance has occurred.

Notes

1. Faye A. Axford, To Lochaber Na Mair, 1986, p. 41
2. Ibid., p. 31
3. Nancy M. Rice, Letter to Terrentina, 1868
4. Nancy M. Rice, Last Will & Testament, January 23, 1880
5. James M. Schmidt, Notre Dame and the Civil War, 2010, p. 109
6. Wilson D. Miscamble, C.S.C, Go Forth and Do Good, 2003, p. 46
7. Bessie Bradwell, Chicago Historical Society, 1926
8. Bureau County Tribune, April 3, 1874, p. 4
9. Jacob Fetrow, Last Will & Testament, October 14, 1889
10. Bureau County Tribune, July 14, 1893, p. 4
11. Ibid., p. 4
12. Ibid., p. 4
13. H.C. Bradsby, History of Bureau County, Illinois, 1885, p. 130
14. Henry Republican, January 6, 1876
15. Bureau County Tribune, January 17, 1908, p. 1
16. Bureau County Tribune, December 9, 1898, p. 12
17. Bureau County Republican, December 23, 1897, p. 10
18. Robert T. Templeton, Last Will & Testament, January 24, 1865, p. 2
19. Ibid., p. 2
20. Ibid., p. 3
21. University of Notre Dame, Twenty-Fourth Annual Catalogue, 1868, p. 8
22. Illinois Medical Society, The Illinois Medical Journal, 1908, Volume 14, p. 14
23. Bureau County Tribune, December 22, 1893, p. 8
24. Bureau County Tribune, October 10, 1895, p. 8
25. Ibid., p. 8
26. University of Notre Dame, Forty-Second Annual Catalogue,

1886, p. 70

27. Tampico Tornado, December 13, 1884, p. 4

28. George B. Harrington, Past and Present of Bureau County, Illinois, 1906, p. 168-169

About the Author

Timothy A. Schlindwein was raised in Princeton, Illinois. He graduated from Princeton High School and from the University of Notre Dame. His investment career began and continues in Chicago. He frequently returns to Princeton and to Notre Dame.

Timothy Schlindwein, Princeton High School, Class of 1965

Timothy Schlindwein, University of Notre Dame, Class of 1969

www.ingramcontent.com/pod-product-compliance
Lightning Source LLC
LaVergne TN
LVHW091031150826
845672LV00006BA/1769

* 9 7 9 8 9 8 8 6 9 4 1 1 3 *